The current values in this book should be used only as a guide. They are not intended to set prices, which vary from one section of the country to another. Auction prices as well as dealer prices vary greatly and are affected by condition as well as demand. Neither the Author nor the Publisher assumes responsibility for any losses that might be incurred as a result of consulting this guide.

ON THE COVER

Top Left — Golden West Coffee tin. $28.00 – 45.00.
Center — Early postal card of Major Gordon W. Lillie best known as
        Pawnee Bill. $25.00 – 35.00.
Top Right — Plaster poly-chromed bust of Hiawatha. Circa 1900. $95.00 –
        150.00.
Middle Left — Powder flask. $85.00 – 175.00.
Bottom Left — Small bronze of a buffalo on a marble base. $375.00 – 500.00.
Bottom Right — *Alaska and the Klondike Gold Fields*. Published in 1897 by
        the Monroe Book Company of Chicago. $55.00 – 95.00.

Searching For A Publisher?
We are always looking for knowledgeable people considered to be experts within their fields. If you feel that there is a real need for a book on your collectible subject and have a large comprehensive collection contact Collector Books.

Cover Design: Beth Summers
Book Design: Kent Henry

Additional copies of this book may be ordered from:

COLLECTOR BOOKS
P.O. Box 3009
Paducah, Kentucky 42002–3009

$24.95. Add $2.00 for postage and handling.

Copyright: David L. Wilson, 1996

Printed in USA

CONTENTS

ACKNOWLEDGMENTS

A cattle drive on the Old Chisholm trail with one cowboy would have been impossible. Writing an illustrated price guide without the enthusiasm, assistance, and cooperation of others would be a similar undertaking.

First and foremost, I thank my lovely wife, Cindy. She provided wonderful support as did my children, Amanda and Grant.

I also thank Marvin Mangers, the general manager of Harold Warp's Pioneer Village in Minden, Nebraska, for his hospitality and genuine interest in my project. This museum is a living testimony to what can be accomplished in the private sector.

Very special thanks also to Sandi Yoder, executive director of the Stuhr Museum of the Prairie Pioneer in Grand Island, Nebraska. I truly enjoyed my time with her great staff of Gail Stoklasa, Kay Cynova, and Thomas Anderson, director of the museum's research department.

Oh bury me out on the lone prairie
Where the coyotes howl and the wind blows free
And when I die you can bury me
Neath the Western sky
On the lone prairie

⌣ Traditional song ⌢

To My Friend
William "Bodie Bill" Luther
A True Western Character

I first had the pleasure of meeting Bill Luther when I became a member of a Southern California antique gun club. The meetings were always informative and included some incredible displays of antique firearms and Western Americana. Bill and I struck up an immediate friendship in spite of the generation gap. That friendship lasted more than two decades until Bill's very untimely passing. I know that I will never meet another person quite like Bill. We both had great interest in the Old West and when we got together, there was never a lapse in the conversation.

Bill was a well-known collector of just about anything connected to the old frontier. More than that, he was a very special person. He respected all that the American West represents — mighty deeds, triumphs and failures, good and evil, a land of promise and adventure for those brave enough to accept the challenge. He possessed a keen knowledge and excitement about the West. Bill was never happier than when he was searching for relics, visiting ghost town sites, and taking many trips with his wife, Barbara. He enjoyed wearing historically correct clothing on special occasions. I recall watching him once as he proudly marched in a parade at Knott's Berry Farm looking much like Kit Carson.

At one time, he owned the only brick building in the rough old mining camp of Bodie, California. He had a great time portraying the "Bodie Sheriff," much to the delight of tourists. His interest in the history of this legendary ghost town and his enthusiasm for preserving it earned him the name of "Bodie Bill" which he was called by his many friends. As most enthusiasts of the Old West know, the state of California did eventually take over the site and has preserved Bodie as a state park.

Bill was always full of enthusiasm and willing to share a special tale with a friend. He liked to talk about his latest "find" and those awaiting discovery. He was particularly fond of rusty relics, especially guns that were found at historic locations. A Colt Navy, for example, found a few feet under the ground in Old Hangtown, California, could conjure up Bill's imagination like nothing else. When I first had the opportunity to purchase an old Colt .44, it was Bill who carefully checked it over and pronounced it to be a "good one." I know that both of us would have fit right in on the old frontier.

Bill always admired John Wayne and I have the feeling that the Duke and Bill have joined outfits and are swapping stories somewhere in the Great Divide. How I would like to hear some of them!

I feel very fortunate to have known Bill and his wife, Barbara. I'm still looking for another compadre like him to share a few campfires with. As the river of time goes on, I know the Great Spirit made only one.

Adios, friend.

David Wilson has been a collector of Western Americana for about thirty years. He has lived in the states of Missouri, Colorado, Montana, Arizona, California, Washington, and Oregon. Dave is a student of the Old West and has traveled to countless historic locations. He is a ghost town enthusiast and enjoys visiting museums throughout the West. He lived for several years in Placerville (Old Hangtown), California, and had the opportunity to talk with many decendants of pioneer days. The author's personal library of books related to the Old West numbers several thousand. He is the author of *General Store Collectibles* and has recently returned to the West and lives with his family in Oregon.

T he Old West! Have any three words ever inspired more imagination and interest in the American experience? From the era of the mountain men to the last mining frontier in Nevada, the cast of characters that populated the Old West offers a river of material. Homesteaders, American Indians, outlaws, gamblers, soldiers, prospectors, store-keepers, lawmen, soiled doves, Alaskan sourdoughs, gunfighters, heroic women — the list goes on and on.

As a youngster growing up in Ohio, I was captivated by the lure of the Old West. The local movie house provided that American institution known as the Saturday matinee. We were favored with one Hollywood Western after another. Comics dealing with everything from shoot-um-up adventure to classics like The Virginian were widely available. I found myself seeking out new articles and listening to "old-timers" with tales to tell.

As time went on and my interests became refined, I found myself haunting the library shelves to seek out books dealing with more historically accurate accounts of the Old West.

I soon came to the realization that I would have to travel west and see the locations and history first-hand. My first opportunity came after high school graduation. I was offered the opportunity to work for the United State Forest Service in Colorado during the summer and continue on to college in Montana. Luck was with me because the Forest Service location was in the incredibly beautiful mountain town of Crested Butte. I used every free moment to visit a number of ghost towns including Tincup, Gothic, Pitkin, and Animas Forks. Montana provided a treasure-trove of history and I was on the go all the time. From there, I had the good fortune to live in Arizona, Missouri, California, Washington, and Oregon. Trips took me to New Mexico, Texas, Idaho, North Dakota, South Dakota, Utah, Kansas, and Nebraska. If I missed some historic sites and museums along the way, they were few.

The majority of my adult life was spent in the West. Along the way, I found it intriguing to study the true history of the region, became an incurable collector, and developed a true appreciation for the Old West. When I started to collect, there were no specialty shows but there were some incredible antique gun shows. Western collectibles would show up just about anywhere and were generally inexpensive because the major collecting interest at the time was in the related areas of antique guns, knives, and leather goods. I recall attending the Las Vegas shows in the '60s. What merchandise! Specialty shows featuring American West collectibles and related items are presently experiencing significant growth. With the increased demand, the prices have escalated to all-time highs. What is my definition of a great Old West collectible? It can be a collectible with origins in the Old West or an item that represents the Old West and simply provides satisfaction to the collector.

My definition is broad because the collectible spectrum is broad. The number of items available that can clearly be traced to the frontier are rapidly diminishing in number as the prices advance. Many Colt Six-Shooters and Model 1873 Winchesters reside in proud collections but how many of them actually saw service on the frontier? It would be great to possess a Model 1873 Colt Single Action that could be documented as being used in a gunfight in Dodge City, Kansas, but such an item is quite rare, as are guns once owned and used by notable Western characters. For a number of reasons, I feel that any item that represents the Old West in some way certainly qualifies as a potential collectible.

For the most part, I have avoided illustrations of the museum-quality or rare item. Chances for ownership are slim and the prices for such items, if they should become available, place them in the category of elite collectible. As with most collectibles, things become available over time as collectors sell items or they are auctioned by the collector or an estate. Butterfield and Butterfield, for example, is a well-known auction house that has offered some scarce and highly desirable collectibles over the years.

Although most of the Western specialty shows are in the West, there are a growing number of dealers in the East. It can be exciting for the collector to seek out items in areas outside the original frontier. Many pieces with authentic origins in the Old West were transported to other parts of the country over the years. The astute collector may find historically significant documents and other artifacts of the West in virtually every state. In other words, one does not need to live in the West to enjoy this highly satisfying hobby.

Collectibles associated with the Great American West have a very special place in the collecting field and that's what I've attempted to give them.

HOLLYWOOD & THE GREAT AMERICAN WEST

 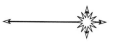
cowboys that mutilated one of their sisters.

17

The Man Who Shot Liberty Valance

A dynamite Western starring James Stewart, John Wayne, and Lee Marvin. The old issues of law and order in a territory growing up keep the viewer's attention in this fast-paced film.

18

Jeremiah Johnson

A man chooses to retreat from civilization and, in the process, becomes a legendary mountain man. The film stunningly depicts the isolation, violence, and self-satisfaction faced in the struggle of being a trapper.

19

Will Penny

Charlton Heston stars as an aging cowboy with limited prospects. He has the misfortune to tangle with a family of nasty rawhiders and crosses paths with them until the deadly finish of the film. There has never been a better performance of a lonely, illiterate cowhand who is still punching cows at an age when most cowboys had long left the range.

20

The Treasure of the Sierra Madre

Although set in 1920s Mexico, Humphrey Bogart, Walter Huston, and Tim Holt turn in outstanding performances as three down-and-outers who meet by chance and decide to look for gold in the dangerous back country. The elements of suspicion, greed, and violence quickly erode their friendship.

These films deal with many aspects of the Western experience. I know they stimulated my interest in collecting and reading books and magazines that offer historical accuracy and demonstrate that the Western expansion was truly incredible! I'm eagerly looking forward to the new films that are now being produced and those that will follow. Thank you, Hollywood!

The Western nostalgic market has exploded. Movie- and television-related collectibles are highly sought after. Everything from 8" x 10" stills, lobby cards, posters, autographs, cap pistols, and other memorabilia are enjoying a booming market. Values can range from a few bucks for a Western poster of recent origin up to a few thousand for a 1926 one-sheet depicting Tom Mix in *No Man's Gold*. Vintage film posters in good condition bring the highest prices but the entire field of movie and TV Western Americana is wide open.

From your old "Pal"

Personal autograph of George "Gabby" Hayes on photo card. $45.00 – 75.00.

HOLLYWOOD & THE GREAT AMERICAN WEST

Hollywood and the media have always made the adventures of the frontier into a larger than life saga. One of the great memories of my childhood was the wonderful opportunity to go to our local movie house on Saturday and be captivated by cowboy heroes and the excitement of their films. Roy Rogers, Gene Autry, John Wayne, Hopalong Cassiday, Randolph Scott, and great character actors such as Andy Devine, Walter Brennan, and George "Gabby" Hayes made the films so enjoyable. My interest in Western movies has never diminished and I'm happy to see Hollywood's recent interest in bringing back the genre. As my tastes and interests became more refined, I found myself carefully observing the authenticity of the sets, costumes, firearms, and locations. For years, it was common for Hollywood film producers to overlook historical accuracy and depict the Old West without the benefit of consultants. We have all witnessed much of the truth coming forward in more recent films and the Model 1892 Winchester doesn't seem to show up as much in circa 1870 films.

It is my feeling that Western films have made the major contribution to the ongoing interest in the Old West and the collector's field. The films stimulate interest in this unique period of history and certainly allow us to escape to yesteryear, if only for some fleeting moments. Hollywood and television have opened up a huge collector's area for a multitude of memorabilia.

I have found over the years that many collectors of Western Americana also enjoy watching a good Western film. For that reason, I decided to open my book with my personal list of my all-time favorites. I don't pretend to be a film critic but I do know what I like. Please bear in mind that these are my personal favorites and excellent cases could be made for many others. My intent is to simply share my thoughts with my readers. I have selected a "top twenty." My list is in no particular order of preference but simply as they

came to mind. I would appreciate hearing from you regarding your personal favorites.

WILSON'S TOP TWENTY WESTERNS

1
Stagecoach
One of the great John Ford Westerns. Who can forget the sweeping vistas of Monument Valley and the performances of John Wayne, Andy Devine, Thomas Mitchell, Claire Trevor, and John Carradine?

2
Ride the High Country
A memorable farewell film starring Randolph Scott and Joel McCrea. The two are hired to transport gold from a raw mining camp. Their values conflict and the story presents these aging stars at their best.

3
Firecreek
This gem of a Western stars James Stewart and Henry Fonda. Stewart is a small-time farmer and part-time sheriff of a town that is on the verge of becoming a ghost town. Henry Fonda is the leader of a band of killers who terrorize Firecreek causing a deadly confrontation.

4
The Gunfighter
Gregory Peck turns in a classic performance as a gunfighter with a big reputation but diminishing heart for the burdens that come along with it. The gunfighter struggles to overcome his past.

5
Monte Walsh
Jack Palance and Lee Marvin play down-on-their-luck cowboys who are trying to find their way in a changing West. The musical score is outstanding and the cowboys look as though they stepped out of a Charles Russell painting.

6
The Searchers

John Wayne and a fine supporting cast turn in great performances. A white girl on the Texas frontier of 1868 has been abducted by Comanches after her family is killed. Wayne dedicates himself to search for her. Many feel that this film is director John Ford's masterpiece.

7
Shane

An immensely beautiful film, stunningly filmed on location in Jackson Hole, Wyoming. The story has a mother lode of memorable moments. Seen through the eyes of a young boy, Shane often transcends every familiar Western element it includes.

8
Heartland

This film was based on the true experiences of Elinore Stewart, who described her frontier life in a series of letters. An outstanding depiction of life on a small ranch and a brave woman's approach to the many rigors of the harsh land.

9
The Ox Bow Incident

A classic look at vigilante justice gone out of control. A posse captures a trio of suspects and ignores the possibility that they are innocent. A great look at social injustice and human nature.

10
The Grey Fox

Richard Farnsworth portrays Canada's gentleman bandit, Bill Miner. A film that won a number of awards. Fresh out of prison after serving 30 years, Miner finds himself released into the twentieth century. Having been a stage robber, Milner begins a new profession — robbing trains.

11
Dances with Wolves

A sweeping story that finds a Civil War soldier with a strong desire to see the Old West before it is gone. He is assigned to an abandoned post and through a number of circumstances, becomes friendly with the Sioux. A compelling look at Indian culture faced with intrusion by the white movement west.

12
Man of the West

Gary Cooper stars with a fine supporting cast. It tells the story of the conflict between two men who were once outlaw partners. One is now reformed and the other is particularly repulsive.

13
Red River

Many consider this to be John Wayne's greatest Western film. Wayne displays many complexities as a self-made cattle rancher on a trail drive. This is an exemplary Western film.

14
McCabe and Mrs. Miller

Warren Beatty stars as a would-be entrepreneur in turn-of-the-century Washington. The story takes place in Presbyterian Church, a thrown-together mining town where desperate people live out a wretched existence. Large mining interests decide to move in and take over with hired killers.

15
3:10 to Yuma

A rancher agrees to take a captured outlaw to Yuma to stand trial, knowing that it may cost his life. The rancher is in need of the reward money to pay the debt on his failing ranch. A compelling story of an ordinary man that must risk everything when no other person will step forward.

16
Unforgiven

An Academy Award winner for Clint Eastwood. A man struggles with his outlaw past and reputation as a killer when a stranger offers him the chance to make some quick money. A group of prostitutes in Big Whiskey, Wyoming, have offered a bounty for killing two

cowboys that mutilated one of their sisters.

17
The Man Who Shot Liberty Valance

A dynamite Western starring James Stewart, John Wayne, and Lee Marvin. The old issues of law and order in a territory growing up keep the viewer's attention in this fast-paced film.

18
Jeremiah Johnson

A man chooses to retreat from civilization and, in the process, becomes a legendary mountain man. The film stunningly depicts the isolation, violence, and self-satisfaction faced in the struggle of being a trapper.

19
Will Penny

Charlton Heston stars as an aging cowboy with limited prospects. He has the misfortune to tangle with a family of nasty rawhiders and crosses paths with them until the deadly finish of the film. There has never been a better performance of a lonely, illiterate cowhand who is still punching cows at an age when most cowboys had long left the range.

20
The Treasure of the Sierra Madre

Although set in 1920s Mexico, Humphrey Bogart, Walter Huston, and Tim Holt turn in outstanding performances as three down-and-outers who meet by chance and decide to look for gold in the dangerous back country. The elements of suspicion, greed, and violence quickly erode their friendship.

These films deal with many aspects of the Western experience. I know they stimulated my interest in collecting and reading books and magazines that offer historical accuracy and demonstrate that the Western expansion was truly incredible! I'm eagerly looking forward to the new films that are now being produced and those that will follow. Thank you, Hollywood!

The Western nostalgic market has exploded. Movie- and television-related collectibles are highly sought after. Everything from 8" x 10" stills, lobby cards, posters, autographs, cap pistols, and other memorabilia are enjoying a booming market. Values can range from a few bucks for a Western poster of recent origin up to a few thousand for a 1926 one-sheet depicting Tom Mix in *No Man's Gold*. Vintage film posters in good condition bring the highest prices but the entire field of movie and TV Western Americana is wide open.

Personal autograph of George "Gabby" Hayes on photo card. $45.00 – 75.00.

WESTERN FILMS — QUOTES

"When in doubt, make a western."
 — John Ford (Hollywood director)

"You can't fight something as big and important as Western Union."
 — Randolph Scott, *Western Union,* 1941

"The Western remains, I suppose, America's distinctive contribution to the film."
 — Arthur Schlesinger, *Show,* 1963

"Rooster was a mean old bastard, a one-eyed, whiskey-soaked, sloppy old son-of-a-bitch, just like me."
 —John Wayne as Rooster Cogburn in *True Grit*

"In the end you end up dying all alone on a dirty street. And for what? For nothing."
 — Gary Cooper, *High Noon,* 1952

"My heart soars like an eagle."
 — Chief Dan George, *Little Big Man,* 1970

"I want to see the frontier ... before it's gone."
 — Kevin Costner, *Dances with Wolves*

"Every day above ground's a good day."
 — Bruce Dern, *Posse,* 1975

"Next time you hang a man, you better make damn sure you get a look at his face!"
 —- Clint Eastwood, *Hang 'Em High,* 1967

Gregory Peck, *The Stalking Moon,* 1968. 8" x 10" photo. $4.00 – 8.00.

Early sepia-toned 8" x 10" photograph of Randolph Scott. $8.00 – 15.00.

How can any Western fans ever forget these two great actors? Chief Dan George and Glenn Ford. 8" x 10" photograph. $5.00 – 10.00.

20th Century-Fox presents
THE CULPEPPER CATTLE CO.

72/8

Excellent movie still photo clearly illustrating attention to authentic cowboy dress. You can't determine if they have just finished a trail drive or are about to begin! *The Culpepper Cattle Co.*, 1972. 8" x 10". $5.00 – 10.00.

Lobby sheet from *The Tall Texan* with Lloyd Bridges, Lee J. Cobb, Marie Windsor, and Luther Adler. $5.00 – 10.00.

Lobby sheet depicting Tim McCoy in *Texas Wildcats*. $7.00 – 12.00.

What a great line-up of Old West characters. From left to right – Jack Elam, Ernest Borgine, and Strother Martin. *Hannie Caulder*, 1972. 8" x 10" movie still. $5.00 – 10.00.

A tense moment during the trail drive. *The Culpepper Cattle Co.*, 1972. 8" x 10" lobby photo. $5.00 – 10.00.

Lobby sheet depicting Bob Steele in *Westward Bound* with Ken Maynard. Bob Steele was one of the giants of the "B" Westerns and later played a number of character roles. $7.00 – 12.00.

Signed photograph of Ken Curtis during his *Gunsmoke* days. 8" x 10" photo. $25.00 – 35.00.

Lobby sheet depicting Johnny Mack Brown in *Six Gun Gospel*. $7.00 – 12.00.

Raymond Massey about to experience frontier justice in *Santa Fe Trail*. 1940, 8" x 10" movie still. $3.00 – 5.00.

Lobby sheet for *I Shot Jesse James* featuring Preston Foster, Barbara Britton, and John Ireland. $7.00 – 12.00.

A tense saloon scene from the classic film, *Shane*, 1953. 8" x 10" lobby photo. $7.00 – 12.00.

A scene from *Twenty Mule Team* with Wallace Berry, Leo Carillo, Ann Baxter, and Noah Beary, Jr., 1940. 8" x 10" movie still. $2.00 – 4.00.

 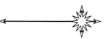

John Wayne and Walter Brennan in one of the greatest Western films ever made, *Red River*. 1948, 8" x 10" movie still. $8.00 – 15.00.

To a man my age, the future doesn't mean much, unless you're talking about next week.

⌐: Richard Farnsworth as *The Grey Fox* :⌐

HOMESTEADING COLLECTIBLES

With the end of the Civil War, America looked to the Western territories for expansion. The promise of free land coupled with exaggerated claims of how easy it was to farm and ranch in the West, brought settlers by the thousands. Most of the frontier was populated by homesteaders and others afire with the pioneer spirit. For that reason, there are many more collectibles available in this area than any other. Pioneers made every effort to take as many comforts of home with them as possible. Musical instruments, china, clocks, stoves, and countless other items were placed into wagons for the trek West. As the burdens of the trail took a toll, many treasured items were discarded along the way. In spite of that, wagon loads of personal property survived the trip and were vital to the establishment of home after home.

The isolation and loneliness of the frontier caused many homesteaders to seek some comfort in their personal and familiar belongings. One only has to take a look at places like Nebraska, Montana, and North Dakota to have a strong feeling for what life must have been like in the early days. Human relationships were scarce and many settlers left their relatives behind. There were few places to go and the hardships of making a living prevented much travel. Occasional trips to the closest general store were eagerly looked forward to. In addition to picking up needed supplies, there were opportunities to talk with neighbors and pick up the latest news. The harsh winters intensified the isolation.

Although the popular conception is that the frontier came to an end about 1890 because there were no new lands to discover, many people in the West continued to live under primitive conditions far into the twentieth century. Kerosene lamps and wood-burning stoves were necessary for many years and continue to be used today.

Homesteading collectibles offer an unlimited area. Just a few of the items taken west were iron stoves, furniture, lanterns, spyglasses, blankets, quilts, water kegs, butter churns, trunks, ox yokes, tools, candle molds, sewing machines, and patented medicines. This area offers a treasure trove of collectibles.

A Conestoga wagon. It is estimated that between 1830 and 1880 more than a million covered wagons crossed the Alleghenies and passed on out to the fertile prairies beyond. A genuine Conestoga wagon would command a "rare item" price.

The interior of a typical covered wagon. The chairs would be valued at $95.00 – 150.00. The trunks $175.00 – 235.00 for the large one and $135.00 – 175.00 for the smaller flat-topped trunk. The pots have a value of $45.00 – 85.00.

An original photo of an early general store in Nebraska. One can see that the variety of goods was very limited and tended to be basic. However, mail was very important as indicated by the large postal area. $45.00 – 60.00.

A pioneer campfire. This is much as it would have looked on the trip overland. The wagons have a value in the $1,750.00 – 2,500.00 range.

Buckboard seat that is now being used as a household seat. $275.00 – 425.00.

Large wagon wheel. $75.00 – 150.00.

Buggy whips. $25.00 – 75.00.

An assortment of buggy whips. $25.00 – 75.00.

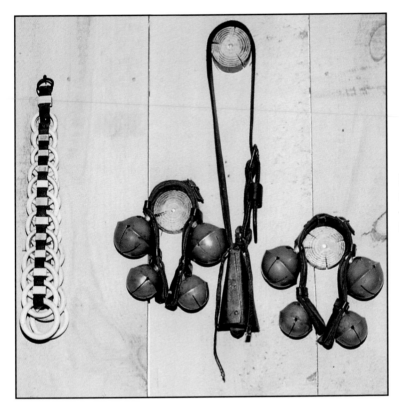

Harness bells. $35.00 – 65.00.
Cow bell with leather strap. $55.00
– 75.00. Celluloid harness section.
$12.00 – 22.00.

Strands of sleigh bells.
$75.00 – 300.00.

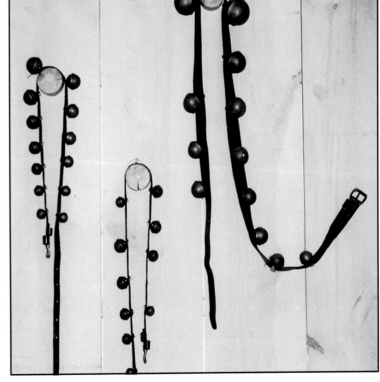

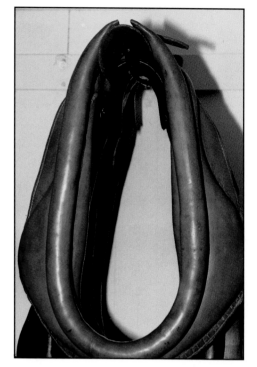

A leather horse collar in "as new" condition. $75.00 – 135.00.

Horse collar. $45.00 – 75.00.

Horse collars. $45.00 – 75.00.

Distance was the enemy, not Indians or crossings or weather or thirst or plains or mountains, but distance, the empty awesome face of distance.

～ A.B. Guthrie, The Way West ～

Single trees.
$15.00 – 32.00.

A large ox yoke.
$175.00 – 300.00.

Another large ox yoke.
$175.00 – 350.00.

Tethering weights for horses. $30.00 – 125.00.

Powder horn with leather shot bag and original strap. $225.00 – 425.00.

Sometimes we found the bones of men bleaching beside their broken-down and abandoned wagons. The buzzards and coyotes, driven away by our presence from their horrible feasting, hovered just out of reach.

⌣: Luzena Wilson, 1849 :⌣

A hide-covered trunk. This type of trunk was used by pioneers as they went west. Good examples are becoming increasingly difficult to find. $325.00 – 475.00.

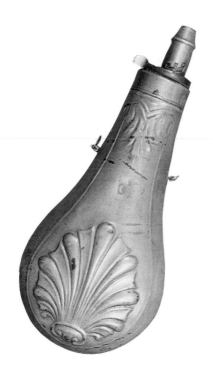

Powder flask. $85.00 – 175.00.

Powder Horn. $75.00 – 225.00. Examples with historical significance or original engravings command much higher prices.

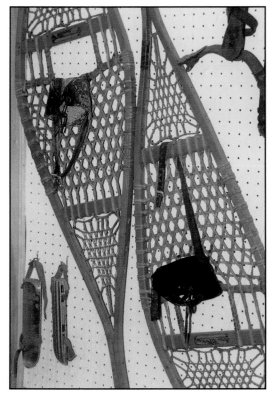

Rawhide lace snow shoes. $150.00 – 225.00. Skates. $65.00 – 125.00.

Wooden bucket. $45.00 – $85.00.

Harness maker's bench. $175.00 – $275.00.

Livestock shears. $22.00 – $45.00.

Wooden butter churn. $135.00 – $215.00.

Deluxe butter churn. $275.00 – $325.00.

Close-up of The Bent Wood Churn. $275.00 – $325.00.

A variety of washboards. These eased the burden of washing clothes but still made it an unpleasant task. $25.00 – 75.00.

A large Niagara Ball Bearing Clothes Mangle. $175.00 – 235.00.

A variety of carpet beaters. $25.00 – 85.00.

The wilderness ever opened the gate of escape to the poor, the discontented and the oppressed...beyond the Alleghanies was freedom.... Thus the demand for land and the love of wilderness drew the frontier ever onward.

Frederick Jackson Turner, *The Significance of the Frontier in American History*

Copper cooking pot. $135.00 – 165.00.

Trivets are a very interesting collector's area. There are so many types! $22.00 – 75.00.

Trivets. They also were called spiders or footmen. When used to hold the pan under the spit, they were called cats or crickets. There are many varieties. $22.00 – 75.00. Exceptional examples will bring higher prices.

A portable pantry. $225.00 – 400.00

A "Quick Time" cook stove. $225.00 – 425.00.

A variety of sad irons. $35.00 – 125.00.

A good quality cook stove. This is a later model. Note the temperature gauge on the door. $475.00 – 1,100.00.

A heavily nickeled cook stove with warming shelf. $850.00 – 1,700.00.

Cook stove with warming oven. $450.00 – 1,250.00. Stoves that have been completely reconditioned demand prices at the higher range. Those that are more ornate bring even higher prices.

Cast-iron stove. This type would have been used in such places as express offices, general stores, schools, and other commercial establishments. $425.00 – 725.00.

A Bellwood stove with embossed eagle on the door. $275.00 – 400.00.

Cast-iron cooking pot and kettle. These were frequently used by overland travelers. $45.00 – 85.00.

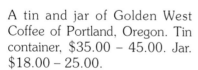
Cast-iron pots and kettles. $45.00 – 85.00.

A tin of Buckingham Cut Plug Smoking Tobacco that was found in Cripple Creek, Colorado. Beautiful graphics. $25.00 – 75.00.

A tin and jar of Golden West Coffee of Portland, Oregon. Tin container, $35.00 – 45.00. Jar. $18.00 – 25.00.

A pitcher and bowl set. Such fine items were often packed and made the trip west. $135.00 – 225.00.

A shaving mug cabinet from a frontier barber shop. The case has a value of $425.00 – 750.00. The mugs will range from $35.00 to several hundred for occupational mugs.

Shaving mugs. $35.00 – 125.00.

 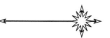

A variety of straight razors. $8.00 – 32.00.

Toilet Glycerin by Elysian Mfg. Co. of Detroit. Bottles of this product made their way west. $25.00 – 35.00.

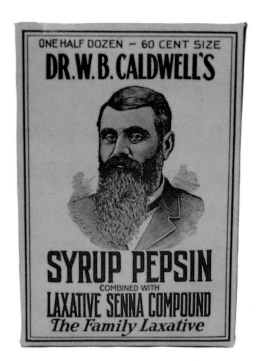

Dr. W. B. Caldwell's Syrup Pepsin was a big seller in the West. This box contained one half dozen bottles at 60¢ per bottle. $75.00 – 135.00.

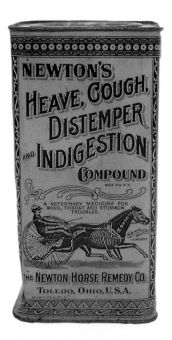

Horses in the Old West developed problems and Newton's Heave, Cough, Distemper and Indigestion Compound was there to be of service. $75.00 – 125.00.

Early pioneer clothing. The bonnet is a replica but the dress is original. $85.00 – 135.00.

A hoop skirt. $65.00 — 125.00.

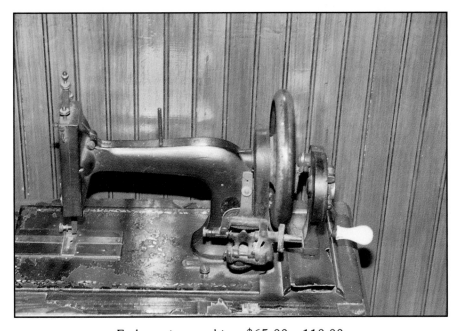

Early sewing machine. $65.00 – 110.00.

An early Minnesota Sewing Machine. Original condition. $95.00 – 135.00.

Early Singer Sewing Machine. Outstanding condition with original gold decals. $275.00 – 375.00.

General Note: A sewing machine in a pioneer home was highly prized. Much of the clothing was made and not "store bought."

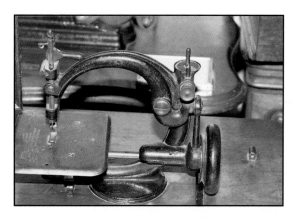

A very early sewing machine. This one could have been easily packed for the trip west. $85.00 – 135.00.

Early sewing machine. $75.00 – 125.00.

40 miles from wood
40 miles from water
40 miles from hell
God bless our home.

Sign on an Arizona ranch house, circa 1900

An early stringed instrument that could be enjoyed at the homestead. $125.00 – 225.00.

An instrument that graced a lot of pioneer campfires and dances. The fiddle appeared early in the Old West. As a matter of fact, a 49er gold rush town in California was given the name "Fiddletown." $65.00 – 400.00.

An early organ. Deluxe finish. These do not have a great deal of functional value today so they can be purchased reasonably. $375.00 – 750.00.

For those who wanted music without being musically inclined, this hand organ was the answer! Just turn the handle and there is instant music. $275.00 – 475.00.

 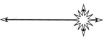

An authentic log cabin. There is strong interest by a number of collectors in purchasing cabins and erecting them at a location of their choice. The basic charge can run from a few hundred dollars to several thousand depending on size, condition, historical significance, and other factors.

The temperature was 122 degrees in the shade, the drinking water was 86 degrees, and the butter poured like oil.

Martha Summerhayes, *Vanished Arizona*, 1874

THE MINING FRONTIER, SALOONS & GAMBLING

From California to the Klondike, from the mountains of Colorado to the deserts of Nevada, the mining frontier left few areas of the West unexplored. When a "diggins" or tent city was established, it was not long before enterprising souls recognized the need for diversions. Hard-working prospectors heartily welcomed the addition of a saloon that offered strong drinks and games of chance. With all of the back-breaking toil day after day, there was little opportunity for some fun. A saloon was the place to go.

Where miners prospered, saloons and gambling halls prospered. Without question, saloons were important for early gold and silver camps. During the heyday of Silverton, Colorado, notorious Blair Street boasted 40 saloons and dance halls and 27 gambling halls. In Ouray, Colorado, the first building was a saloon. Often, business was started with just one barrel of whiskey and little or nothing in the way of fixtures. As a mining camp developed, a saloon and gambling hall would import fancy bars, ornate lighting, nude oil paintings, and a wide variety of gambling equipment. Anything necessary to keep the prospector's thoughts off his poke and tomorrow's work.

It was possible for proprietor's to purchase jug whiskey at 25¢ a gallon. In mining towns during boom times, it was not uncommon to charge a customer as much as 25¢ a shot.

Today's collector has a remarkable variety of items available in the collecting areas of mining, saloons, and gambling. Mining collectibles can include, but are not limited to, stock certificates, gold pans and pokes, lighting devices, scales, ore cars, tools, early photos, signs, assay reports and other paper items, and early books.

Saloon and gambling collectibles can include bottles, gambling machines, advertising items, saloon paintings, cards, card trimmers, gaming boards, trays, flasks, gambler's weapons including dirks, bowie knives, and firearms, roulette wheels, faro tables, dice, cheating devices, and tin advertising trays.

Prospecting, gambling, and patronizing saloons were valued activities in the Old West but not always in that order. For some of the early prospectors, whiskey and gambling held an esteemed place, often ahead of food, women, and even gold. Some early mining camps suggest the strong connection between prospecting and the vices. You Bet, Jackpot, Poker Flats, Whiskey Diggings, and Whiskeytown, to name just a few.

Collectors can be modern-day prospectors as they search for relics related to mining, saloons, and gambling!

Photograph of James Marshall, credited with the discovery of gold at Coloma, California, in 1848. Marshall was a carpenter under the employ of John Sutter. He profited very little from his discovery. Rare. $700.00 – 1,500.00.

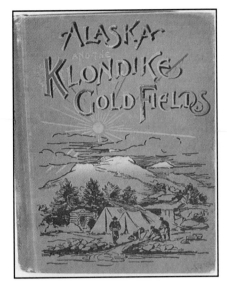

Alaska and the Klondike Gold Fields published in 1897 by the Monroe Book Company of Chicago. Includes chapters entitled "Strike It Rich on the Klondike"; "Women at the Mines"; "How to Get There"; "Resumé of Mining Laws"; and "Gold Mining In Alaska." Includes maps. Books such as this one prompted countless numbers to seek their fortune. $55.00 – 95.00.

Miner's lighting devices. $25.00 – 65.00.

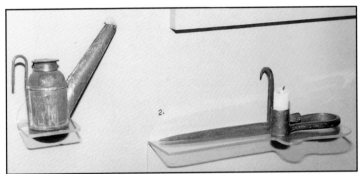

Gold prospector's pan. Used in all of the gold rushes to find "color." Part of every prospector's outfit. Still in use today. $75.00 – 135.00. Early specimens are becoming difficult to locate.

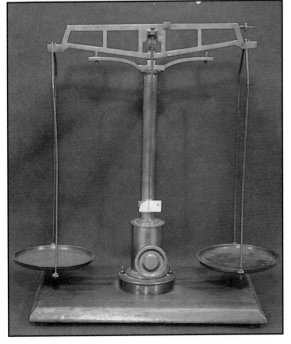

Early gold scales with original pans. Used in the mother lode of California. $400.00 – 650.00.

Gold mining is Nature's great lottery scheme. A man may work a claim for many months, and be poorer at the end of the time than when he commenced; or he may take out thousands in a few hours. It is a mere matter of chance.

∽ Dame Shirley ∾

Gold scales with original box. $175.00 – 250.00.

Early gold scales from Amador City, California. $225.00 – 350.00.

Prospector's pack saddle. Used throughout the Old West. Could hold a remarkable quantity of supplies. $135.00 – 225.00.

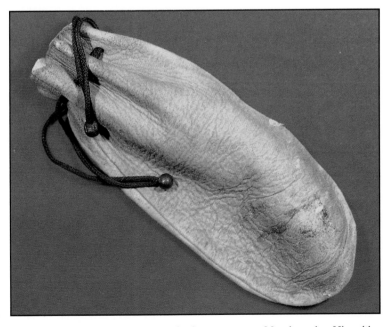

Large buckskin gold poke with draw strings. Used in the Klondike gold rush. $110 – 135.00.

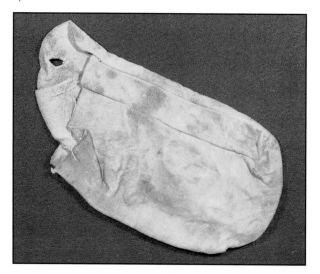

✧ ✷✷ ✧

Show us the gold. Show us the gold.

✧ Seattle crowd as a steamship returns from
the Alaska gold rush, 1897 ✧

Buckskin gold poke. $25.00 – 38.00.

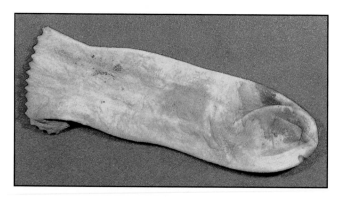

Small buckskin gold poke. California mother lode.
$45.00 – 70.00.

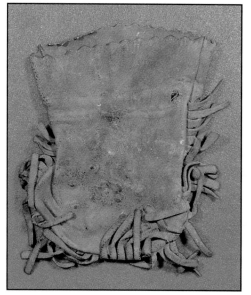

Fringed buckskin gold poke with floral
design. $55.00 – 85.00.

Two derbies hanging on an oak rack. Derbies were frequently worn by gamblers and saloon patrons. $35.00 – 85.00 each.

Gambler's carpet bag. Professional gamblers in the Old West were frequently on the move. Personal belongings could be moved quickly in such a bag. $125.00 – 225.00.

Gambler's handmade linen vest. Such vests sometimes came equipped with a few "extra" pockets. $125.00 – 250.00.

Roulette wheel. They were produced in a variety of sizes and very well made. Large sums of money were often lost or won on one turn of the roulette wheel. $550.00 – 1200.00.

Dealing boxes used in faro and other card games. They were invented to prevent cheating. Needless to say, enterprising gamblers soon were able to utilize them to their advantage. $55.00 – 85.00.

Faro table, circa 1890. The most common suit that the layout was manufactured in was spades, with the second most common being clubs. $2,250.00 – 4,500.00.

The New Century gambling machine. Top-grade cabinet. $10,000.00 – 15,000.00.

Roulette machine. A roulette game's color-keyed slots took quarter bets for payouts up to $10. Very ornate. $10,000.00 – 15,000.00.

 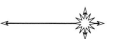

The Victor upright slot machine. Put in your coin, crank the handle, and take your chance. Fancy oak cabinet. $5,500.00 – 8,500.00.

⌁∗∗⌁

All the chances are with the man who owns the house.
⌁ Edward Chase, the gambling king of Denver ⌁

An oak-encased game of chance with encased bicycle. $1,400.00 – 2,250.00.

Roulette wheel with gaming table. Original cost about $185. $5,500.00 – 8,500.00.

A close-up of the top of the gaming board.

A casekeeper. Operated by an employee of the house and used to allow the players to know which cards had come out of the dealing box. Made of fine woods and the "beads" or counters were often made out of ivory. $650.00 – 1,000.00.

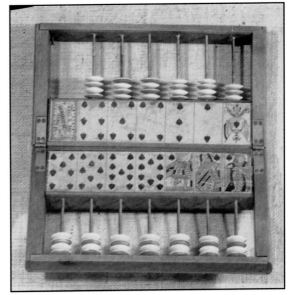

Whiskey Bottle, Hayner Whiskey. Fluted top & bottom, circa 1890. $15.00 – 30.00.

Liquor bottle with original label. $65.00 – 85.00.

Oak saloon back bar. $3,200.00 – 5,000.00.

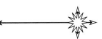

A saloon brass spittoon. A fixture in just about every saloon in the West. $75.00 – 140.00. Collector alert — This item has been frequently reproduced. Look for original patina, markings, and wear.

A whiskey cask with fancy mounting. $235.00 – 350.00.

Saloon serving tray, circa 1900. Depicts beautiful buxom lady with roses. Caption is "Beauty Contest." $175.00 – 325.00.

The cheapest and easiest way to become an influential man and be looked up to by the community at large, was to stand behind a bar, wear a cluster-diamond, and sell whiskey.

∾ Mark Twain ∾

Pale Orange Bitter's bottle. Original label. $75.00 – 125.00.

⊶ ✳✳ ⊷
The Comstock is the mother of silver mining in America.
⊶ Dan De Quille on Comstock Lode, Nevada, 1889 ⊷

Fancy oak-encased clock. Clocks of this type were frequently used in saloons but often kept out of the direct sight of patrons. After all, it was not good business to remind customers of the time. $450.00 – 675.00.

King Alfred Cigar lighter with clock. There was nothing like a good "seegar" and the better saloons offered them. $375.00 – 650.00.

Rolled-tin lithographed illustration entitled "Carmen." One can see how this would be a great item for the saloon keeper to hang on the wall. The customers certainly appreciated it! Circa 1900. $235.00 – 450.00.

Another rolled-tin lithographed illustration of a beautiful lady entitled "Griselda." These were often given to saloons by distributors of spirits and hung on the wall. This particular illustration is a stock item and was frequently used. Circa 1900. $125.00 – 250.00.

HORSE TRANSPORTATION IN THE OLD WEST

 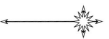

There is a growing interest in original horse-drawn wagons, buggies, coaches, and sleds that saw service in the early days of the American West. The dry air of the West has served to preserve numerous examples and for years the landscape was dotted with the remains of buggies and wagons as they passed their time in the harsh weather. Many others were kept in barns and storage sheds "for old times sake" with the advent of the automobile. It can be both challenging and gratifying for the collector to locate one of these great relics of the past and do the necessary repairs to bring one up to top condition. Most of them were made extremely well and intended to last for years.

There are a scattered number of old-time craftsmen that are quite capable of doing outstanding restoration work. The collector can be thankful for the American institution of the parade. This has resulted in people seeking out old horse-drawn vehicles for that special moment as the parade heads up main street. A large variety of horse-drawn vehicles in great shape can be a marvelous happening at a parade or other special event.

I have a friend in California that provides wagons and other related items to the Hollywood movie industry when these are called for. He derives great satisfaction from the business. Several years ago, an original Wells Fargo stagecoach came on the market. This one was very special because it was in "retired" condition and still had the dust of the California mother lode on it. That is what attracted the eventual purchaser. He commented to me that he did not intend to do anything in the way of restoration. He wanted to leave it just the way it was found and savor all the wear and tear not to mention the history!

Lack of transportation in the Old West often had harsh results. The frontier doctor on his way to a ranch to tend to the injured and ill; the freighter bringing crucial supplies to a mining town; the cattleman delivering feed to his herd in the midst of winter storms; and the homesteader heading to town for provisions all counted on their buggies and wagons. Every town of any size had a much-needed blacksmith to help keep things moving. A Saturday visit to the general store by farmers and ranchers was a social custom. A child was often excited by the words "let's hitch the horses to the wagon and go to town."

Values of horse-drawn vehicles can range from a few hundred dollars to several thousand depending on scarcity and desirability. This chapter will bring you a cross section of what is available. There was a remarkable variety made by manufacturers and it seems there is always something different turning up. They stand as an amazing tribute to the Old West.

During the period that buggies and carriages were most in need in the West, manufacturers were discovering techniques to reduce the cost. Specifically, mass production and the use of standard parts were emerging and makers could purchase wheels, axles, lamps, springs, top fittings, whip sockets, and other parts from specialty shops. The carriage builder became more of an assembler and finisher.

Buggies and carriages are still being manufactured for sale in the United States. For example, the latest catalog of the Cumberland General Store of Crossville, Tennessee, has a spring wagon available for $4,725, a surrey with the fringe on top for $4,650, and a buckboard for $4,750. There is also a delivery wagon listed for $4,375. There are also those that offer restoration services and have the ability to bring early horse-drawn vehicles to near mint condition. It certainly is enjoyable to preserve a part of the historic Old West!

I have made it a point to provide my readers with close-ups of the horse-drawn vehicles illustrated in this chapter. This permits the opportunity to truly appreciate this very colorful and necessary part of the old frontier.

The Conestoga wagon. It was built lower to the center so supplies would not fall out while crossing rugged mountains. $7,500.00 – 12,000.00.

Take good care of your trains — keep things in order, oiled, etc. No traveling on Sunday unless in search of water or grass or the health of your camp requires it.

⌣ "Instructions to Freighters" Russell & Waddell, Leavenworth City, K.T., 1857 ⌣

Wells Fargo stagecoach. Bright red Concords from New England carried cowboys, miners, merchants, actors, gamblers, and farmers throughout the West. They played a major role in the settlement and development of the Old West. $50,000.00 +.

The first stage coach reached Denver in 1859. Coaches such as this one were drawn by four or six galloping steeds. The ruggedly built Concord coach was most popular in mountainous terrain, while the lightweight coaches were preferred in flat country. $25,000.00 +.

A heavily-built freight wagon was a common sight in the Old West. In the 1860s one firm alone, Russell, Majors & Waddell, required the use of 6,000 wagons in operating a freighting company over the Oregon Trail. $950.00 – 1,600.00.

Spring wagon. Equipped with optional or pole shafts for use with one or two horses. $2,200.00 – 3,400.00.

Spring wagon. It cost $54.50 in 1907. $900.00 – 1,700.00.

 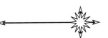

The buckboard. This rig compares with the present day van. The seats were easily moved or removed to make room for freight, supplies, and other items. $1,250.00 – 1,850.00.

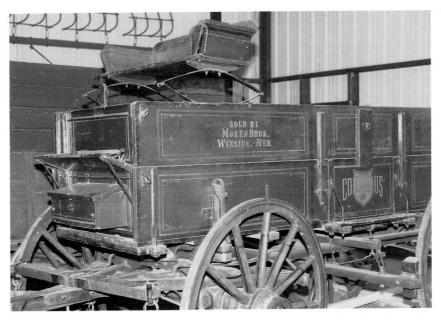

Columbus ranch & farm wagon. Sold by Moses Brothers, Winside, Nebraska. $1,500.00 – 2,500.00.

A typical ranch utility wagon. In wide use throughout the Old West. This wagon permitted delivery of feed to cattle and other livestock. $950.00 – 1,450.00.

Studebaker ranch & farm wagon. Manufactured by the Studebaker Brothers who went on to manufacture automobiles. $1,250.00 – 2,750.00.

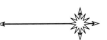
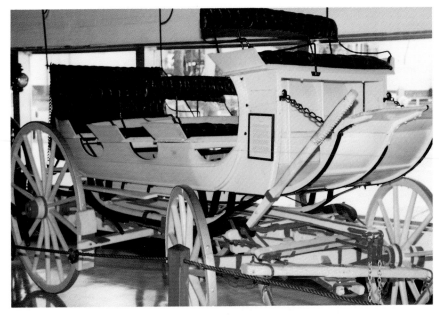

Yellowstone wagon, 1880 – 1916. Made of Abbott-Downing of Concord, New Hampshire, they were pulled by four horses. Between 1880 and 1916, approximately 307,000 visitors were hauled through Yellowstone Park in 165 wagons similar to this one. $5,000.00 – 8,500.00.

Surrey. It could handle the driver and three passengers. $2,200.00 – 3,500.00.

A surrey. These could generally be rented at the local livery stable and were quite popular for a Sunday ride. $2,100.00 – 2,900.00.

✥✥

Travel, travel, travel — nothing else will take you to the end of your journey; nothing is wise that does not help you along; nothing is good for you that causes a moments delay.

— Marcus Whitman, Oregon Trail, 1843

A spring buggy with top. $2,400.00 – 3,200.00.

70

This type of buggy was often used by the local doctor as he made his rounds to rural areas. This one was used in Nebraska. $1,350.00 – 2,600.00.

Extension-top phaeton. Iron-frame and leather-covered fenders to help protect the carriage and occupants from mud. In lowering the top, it was first necessary to insert the pivots of the front set of top bows into the eyes on the forward bow of the rear set. $2,800.00 – 4,000.00.

A depot wagon. Frequently used around train stations to move luggage and small items of freight. $900.00 – 1,300.00.

Hotel coach. Marked "Hotel Transfer Lines" and used for moving guests and their luggage to and from the hotel. Many of them had painted scenes on them as this one does. $5,500.00 – 9,000.00.

A rural free delivery mail wagon. By 1910, there were thousands of these vehicles on the roads of America, including the West. $2,400.00 – 4,500.00.

Another U.S. mail rural route wagon. It was designed to be comfortable in bad weather and bring much-desired mail and packages to the rural areas. $2,400.00 – 4,500.00.

 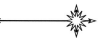

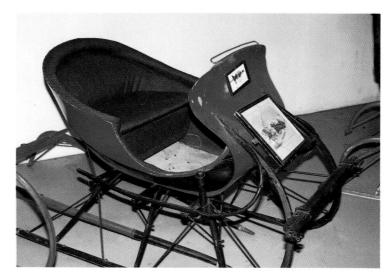

The sleigh. A small two-passenger model. Weather conditions in many parts of the West required its usage. $725.00 – 1,350.00.

Pioneer Ice Company. Ice was put up during the winter months and sawed into cakes of 50 or 100 pounds. With no other means of cooling food items, ice was a valuable commodity. $3,200.00 – 5,500.00.

Horse-drawn hearse. Hearses very similar to this one were in use even in the remote mining towns of the West. Bodie, California, claimed to be the "toughest town in the West," had many occasions to use the hearse. Gunfights and stabbings were common. $3,500.00 – 6,000.00.

ADVERTISING, PHOTOS, HISTORICAL
DOCUMENTS & GENERAL EPHEMERA

Collecting early advertising items featuring illustrations of the Old West, photographs, historical documents, and general ephemera probably offers the greatest variety and availability of any collecting area. There are literally thousands of items available and there is always the opportunity to make a great discovery. This category of collectible can be found from Maine to Montana.

ADVERTISING

The romance of the Old West quickly captured the imagination of advertisers and illustrators "back East." American Indians, cowboys, prospectors, cowgirls, buffalo, and outdoor scenes were quickly adapted to broadsides, posters, trade cards, calendars, postal cards, and used to advertise products from tobacco to soap. The era from the 1880s to the 1920s produced an incredible variety of collectibles. Some of the best examples of advertising signs and posters have been elevated to an art form in today's market. Auction prices in recent years have supported the rise of top advertising items to an art form.

PHOTOS

Photos of the Old West fall in several categories:

1. Notable historical figures such as Buffalo Bill Cody and Geronimo.
2. American Indians and Cowboys.
3. U.S. Army on the Western Frontier.
4. Mining.
5. Homesteading scenes and life in the West.
6. Saloons and Gambling.
7. Town views.
8. Landscapes.
9. Transportation.

Early original photographs can run the entire spectrum of price ranges. A fairly common landscape view, for example, with nothing unusual about it can sell for as low as a few dollars. On the other hand, the sky's the limit if an unknown photograph of Wild Bill Hickok should surface. If the photo was taken just prior to his death in Deadwood, South Dakota, one can only speculate on the potential price. I recall visiting an antique shop in Long Beach, California, several years ago. The owner was aware of my interest in Western items and had just acquired several photographs of Apache Indians. I was immediately interested in examining them and noted that they were stamped on the back with the photographer's name, Randell-Arizona Territory. One of the photos was Geronimo! I was thankful for all of the reading and studying that I had done over the years. I recognized Geronimo as well as Nana and some others. To the shop owner, they were just some American Indian photographs. The asking price reflected his knowledge. Those kind of opportunities are few and far between.

HISTORICAL DOCUMENTS & GENERAL EPHEMERA

The fascinating thing about documents is that they can show up just about anywhere. As postal service became more efficient, letters were sent from the West to friends and relatives in the East in larger numbers. Many of the letters contain wonderful glimpses of life in the Old West. Prospectors, soldiers, and business people found time to take pen in hand and describe their activities.

This area is now showing substantial interest by a growing number of collectors. A record price of $3,600 for a document signed by New Mexico lawman, Pat Garrett, was set at an auction conducted by American West Archives. The document was an 1881 "Sheriff's Account" handwritten and signed by Garrett. Nevada gunman, "Diamondfield" Jack Davis, whose colorful exploits included his avoidance of three hanging dates for allegedly killing two sheepherders during the Nevada/Idaho range wars of the 1890's, was another Old West autograph that commanded a high price. A check signed by him brought $500.

What can bring the Old West back to life better than a letter that was written by a person who experienced it? Old documents are often one-of-a-kind and frequently provide significant historical information as well as simply being interesting in their own right. I have a letter in my collection from a saloon keeper in Pitkin, Colorado, that was written in the 1880s. The letter was sent to his brother in New York attempting to convince him to come west and join in the business. He comments "Never have I made so much money with little work." One wonders if the brother accepted and enjoyed good fortune before Pitkin declined and eventually became a ghost town.

Waybills, diaries, railroad and mining stocks, books, billheads, land grants, broken-bank notes, and letters are just a few of the collecting areas available.

A word of caution is in order. Documents and photographs are among the easiest things in the world to reproduce and for which to find acceptance. Documents can be artificially aged and worn to give the appearance of an original. It is a good practice to do business with recognized dealers or ask for the assistance of a more knowledgeable person before parting with those hard-earned dollars. On the other hand, there are still thousands of more common items that are probably what they appear to be. As with any area of collecting, the more knowledge you possess, the more effective you will be!

Territory of Nebraska. Acting Governor J. Sterling Morton appoints a county commissioner, Omaha City, 1858. $75.00 – 135.00.

77

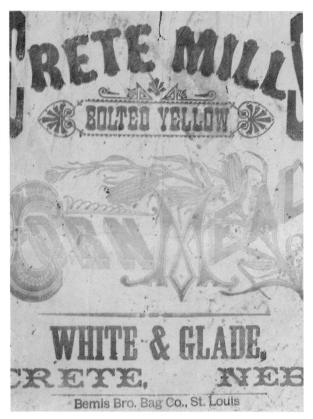

Corn meal bag, Crete Mills, Crete, Nebraska. Circa 1890. $35.00 – 55.00.

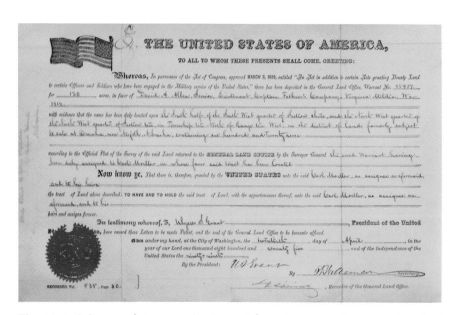

The United States of America land grant for military service. One hundred and twenty acres in Nebraska. Dated 1875, signed by U.S. Grant, President. $325.00 – 625.00.

Nevada Southern Railway Company trustee's certificate.
$22.00 – 32.00.

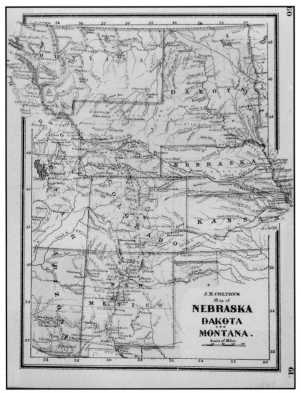

Map of Nebraska, Dakota & Montana. J.H. Colton.
$35.00 – 45.00.

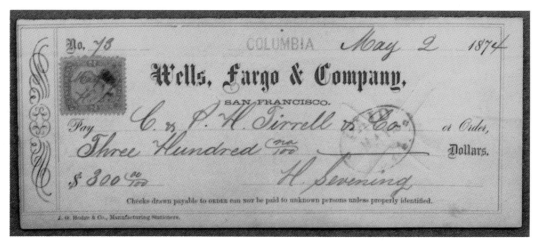

Wells, Fargo & Company, Columbia, California, May 2nd, 1874. Check payable for $300. The old gold camp of Columbia is now a California state park. $28.00 – 45.00.

Johnson Halter. Large simulated horse-head made to advertise the product. Used in harness, tack, and livery shops. $525.00 – 825.00.

Columbia gall cure & healing powder. Horse mounted on the base advertising the product. Made of plaster of Paris. $375.00 – 525.00.

Celluloid ad for The Cudahy Packing Co. of South Omaha, Nebraska. Depicts a Plains Indian and offers "one of these elegant Indian pictures, unmounted, free from advertising with the submission of a metal cap from a jar of Rex Beef Extract. Circa 1899. $150.00 – 225.00.

Turn-of-the-century postal card illustrating a cowgirl sitting on a saloon table with revolver ready. The caption is "Free and Easy." $8.00 – 15.00.

Orico tobacco tin with American Indian lithographed scene. $375.00 – 650.00.

Kickapoo Indian Almanac, 1894. $35.00 – 55.00.

Back cover of the Kickapoo Indian Almanac. Great illustrations of Plains Indian artifacts.

Early postal card of Major Gordon W. Lillie, best known as Pawnee Bill. Involved in Wild West shows with Buffalo Bill Cody. $25.00 – 35.00.

Lithoraphed label for The Round-Up Cigars. $7.00 – 12.00.

Large card with a Western woman proudly sitting with her Winchester. $25.00 – 35.00.

Larger-sized card illustrating a woman of the Wild West with her six gun. $25.00 – 35.00.

Advertising poster for Campbell's Horse Foot Remedy. Illustrations include an American Indian and cowboy. $750.00 – 1,250.00.

84

Discharge from military service. Issued in Austin, Texas, in 1866. $75.00 – 125.00.

Turn-of-the-century postal card depicting and American bison. Post-marked Great Falls, Montana. $8.00 – 12.00.

Union Pacific Land Grant promotional ad, Omaha, Nebraska, 1881. $85.00 – 135.00.

Political poster found in Kansas. McKinley & Roosevelt, circa 1900. $375.00 – 700.00.

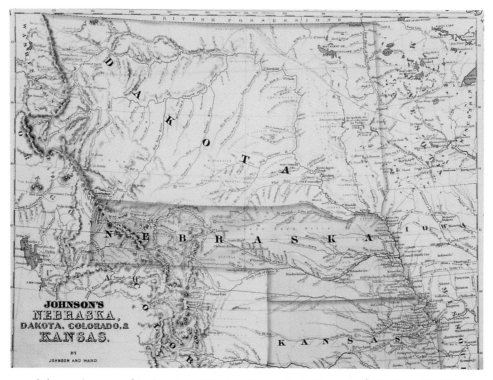

Johnson's map of Nebraska, Dakota, Colorado & Kansas. $45.00 – 60.00.

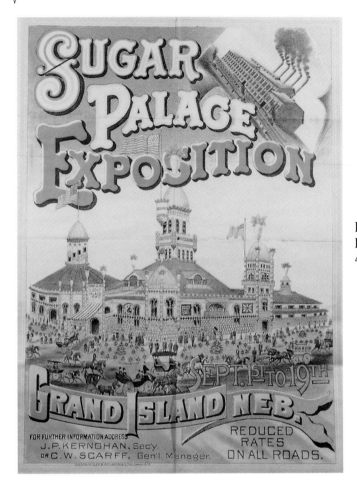

Large Sugar Palace Exposition poster, Grand Island, Nebraska. Beautifully illustrated. $375.00 – 450.00.

Rocky Mountain National Bank, Central City, Colorado, 1874. Check for $34. $22.00 – 35.00.

Frank Leslie's Illustrated Newspaper, 1877. Depicts the Nebraska Sheep Shearing Festival, Beatrice, Nebraska. $27.00 – 38.00.

Railway Officials & Employes (sic) Accident Association insurance policy issued to a customer in Grand Island, Nebraska. Principal amount is $2000 with a weekly indemnity of $10. $12.00 – 22.00.

Large framed photo of Chief Tall Tree. $375.00 – 650.00.

Certificate for five years of faithful service to the Grand Island, Nebraska, Fire Department, dated 1898. $350.00 – 675.00.

Autograph of Buffalo Bill Cody. The inscription reads "True to friend and foe," 1890. $325.00 – 750.00.

Sepia-toned photograph of William Jennings Bryan. Known as the "crusader from the plains," he gave speeches throughout the West and was in favor of free silver. $125.00 – 175.00.

Texas Jack Omohundro, a friend of Buffalo Bill and
noted plainsman. Cabinet photo. $225.00 – 350.00.

Golden West Coffee tin and glass jar, Portland-Seattle. $28.00 – 45.00.

Scarce photo of American Indians displaying their peace medals. $325.00 – 450.00.

The legendary Calamity Jane. Huffman photo, postal card, circa 1900. $10.00 – 18.00.

Small photo of an Idaho hunter, circa 1890. $22.00 – 30.00.

Original cabinet photo of Buffalo Bill Cody taken in Chicago during one of his Wild West shows. Framed in period frame. $325.00 – 550.00.

Portrait of an American Indian, 8" x 10". $155.00 – 275.00.

Large paper advertising sign. Prince Albert Tobacco. Indian series, 20" x 25", circa 1914. $475.00 – 850.00.

Cabinet photo of an American cowboy taken by W.J. Lee during his travels in the Old West. $125.00 – 175.00.

Photo of Apache Indians taken in Arizona, circa 1890. $95.00 – 165.00.

Hunting camp scene captioned "Oregon Bill at Home." $55.00 – 75.00.

❖❖❖

Young skinny wiry fellows, not over eighteen. Must be expert riders willing to risk death daily. Orphans preferred.

❖ Pony Express ad 1860 ❖

Mail Pouch — The Real Man's Choice. One of the series of informative posters used by Mail Pouch. This one is particularly interesting because of the Old West theme. $225.00 – 450.00.

Large photo of an early silent screen actress standing next to a stage-coach and ready for action! Ornate oak frame. $325.00 – 400.00.

A Walla Walla Indian. One of a series by the famed photographer, Curtis. Photogravure. $225.00 – 450.00.

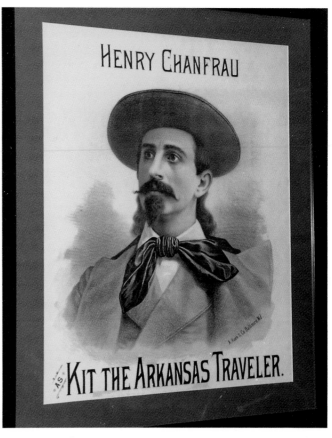

Henry Chanfrau in his role as "Kit The Arkansas Traveler." Actors such as Mr. Chanfrau traveled throughout the West bringing entertainment to the mining and cattle towns. Outstanding early poster. $425.00 – 650.00.

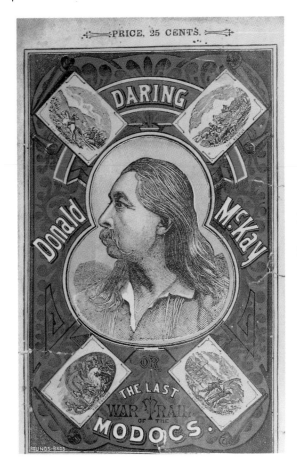

Magazine entitled *Daring Donald McKay or The Last War Trail of the Modocs*. Illustrated scenes depict Daring Donald in action. $27.00 – 35.00.

Poster of a hunter in the Rocky Mountains, circa 1890. $75.00 – 125.00.

Why any man would willingly live in a city, with its infernal stinks and noises, he would never know...when he could come west to God's finest sculptures.

∿ Vardis Fisher, mountain man ∿

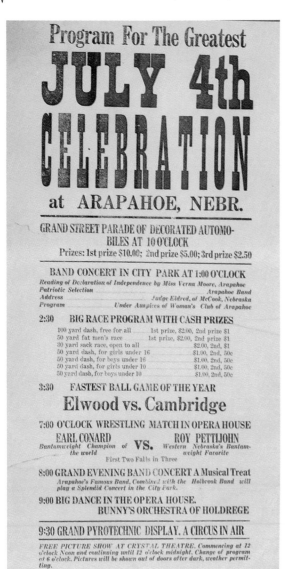

A poster advertising a July 4th celebration at Arapahoe, Nebraska. All kinds of entertainment from races to wrestling. $65.00 – 125.00.

Calendar page for October 1901 illustrating George Armstrong Custer at the Little Big Horn and his "Last Stand." Produced for Armour's Packing Company. $65.00 – 85.00.

Photo of Two Gun White Calf, 8" x 10". $225.00 – 400.00.

⤳✳✳⤶

Everything is quiet in Cimarron (New Mexico).
Nobody has been killed in three days.

⤳ *Las Vegas Gazette* ⤶

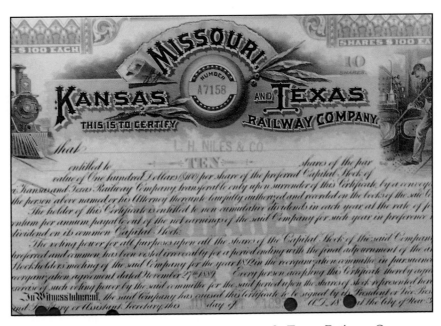

Stock certificate from the Missouri, Kansas & Texas Railway Company, 1895. $15.00 – 27.00.

Lithographed print entitled "U.S. Army Infantry Attacking Snake River Indians Near Owyhee River – 1880." The Werner Company, Akron, Ohio, 1899. $85.00 – 125.00.

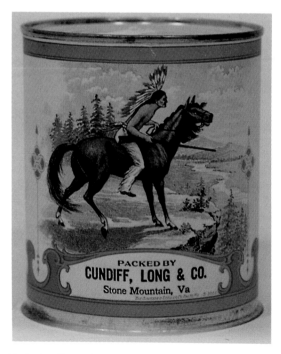

Pohaka Brand Tomatoes packed by Cundiff, Long & Co., Stone Mountain, Virginia, 1906. $15.00 – 20.00.

Buffalo Bill Cody, 8" x 10" portrait, 1907. Cody is said to have called this his favorite photograph of himself. Period frame. $525.00 – 900.00.

WESTERN ART OBJECTS

One certain way to share the Western experience is to collect art focused on the Old West. There truly is an incredible variety available. Starting with some of the masters, artists like Charlie Russell, Frederick Remington, Gerard Curtis Delano, Harold Von Schmidt, Olaf Wieghorst, Will James, Frank Tenney Johnson, Edward Borein, Robert Lindneux, W.H.D. Koerner, Maynard Dixon, Olaf Seltzer, Edgar S. Paxson, Charles Schreyvogel, Frank Reaugh, Harvey Dunn, and Shorty Shope have provided the groundwork for many others that were captivated by the grand panorama of the Great West.

It seems that the early artists have accelerated the development of today's "cowboy artist." The works represent an incredible display of skill coupled with a good understanding of the subject.

Art galleries located in Scottsdale, Arizona, and Jackson Hole, Wyoming, among many others, display something for everyone with a love of the Old West. Specialty shows and auctions also do a brisk business.

There is something special about having an original piece of art hanging from your wall or placed on a desk. Oils, water colors, pen and inks, and sculptures of every description are available. I have a large painting in my study of a California prospector proudly holding a gold nugget. It was painted in 1971 and the artist actually had a friend pose in the Coloma area to capture the history of the mother lode. The costume is true to the era and large California oaks loom in the background as a stream gurgles by. The painting hangs by my desk and warms my spirit when I look at it. For a moment or two, I am transported back in time to the 1850s. It can be exhilarating!

The price range for quality art is extremely wide but fine original pieces can be purchased for reasonable sums. As always, the collector should only purchase something that clearly strikes a chord and will continue to do so. Disposing of artwork is much more difficult than antiques or collectibles in general. Determining fair market value often requires extensive research. Pieces of art are generally consigned to galleries or auction houses for disposal with the resultant fees. The best advice is make certain you love it and be prepared to keep it! There have been substantial increases in value over the years for selective works and many collectors have been very pleased at sale time.

It is best to deal with recognized galleries or collectors that can authenticate a painting for you. Auction houses that present specialty auctions which include Western art will stand behind the works being offered. There is a growing market for fine prints of modern works. This is certainly an option if the collector is unable to afford an original by a particular artist but admires the work. It can be quite satisfying to discover an emerging artist and have the ability to make purchases when the prices are still reasonable.

So great is the attachment of the American artist for the Great West that the output of Western art will continue to flourish.

Nature is the only real teacher of art
Jimmy Swinnerton (Western painter)

 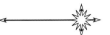

Ambushed by A.R. Tilburne. Tilburne traveled throughout the West making sketches and drawings which served as the basis for his paintings. His father "Nevada Ned" was a close friend of Buffalo Bill. Tilburne died in January, 1965. Oil. $2,500.00 +.

The Fight by A.R. Tilburne. Oil. $2,500.00 +.

A Morning Pitch by A.R. Tilburne. Oil. $2,500.00 +.

William Frederick Cody, *Buffalo Bill*, 1846 – 1917. By A.R. Tilburne. Oil. $5,000.00 +.

The Alert by A.R. Tilburne. Oil. $2,500.00 +.

Guardians of the Herd by A.R. Tilburne. Oil. $2,500.00 +.

Bloomington Land Office, People's Store and Soddy by A.R. Tilburne. Oil. 2,500.00 +.

The Old Elm Creek Stockade by A.R. Tilburne. Oil. $2,500.00 +.

The Promised Land by A.R. Tilburne. Oil. $2,500.00 +.

Gold by A.R. Tilburne. The artist has certainly captured the look of greed and possible violence. Oil. $2,500.00 +.

Bitter Water by A.R. Tilburne. Oil. $2,500.00 +.

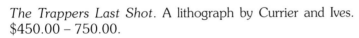

The Trappers Last Shot. A lithograph by Currier and Ives. $450.00 – 750.00.

Indian Camp in Winter by C.M. Ottinger. $2,000.00+.

 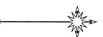

Early lithograph of a gold camp in the Sierra Nevada Mountains of California. Crocker Comapny, San Francisco. $165.00 – 300.00.

·:❋❋:·

A woman can go further with a lipstick than a man can with a Winchester and a side of bacon.

·: Charles Russell, 1925, *More Rawhides* :·

A cowboy serenade, artist unknown. It appears it could have been an illustration. $1,000.00 +.

A lithographed print for Marlin Firearms. It depicts two men leaving camp in their canoe. Circa 1900. $225.00 – 400.00.

California Prospector 1849 by Reuel Deckard. $1,500.00+.

Sitting Bull. A charcoal sketch. Artist unknown. $400.00 – 650.00.

In Arizona nature allures with her gorgeous color then repels with the cruelty of her formations, waterless, barren and desolate.

꞉ Frederick Remington ꞉

 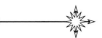

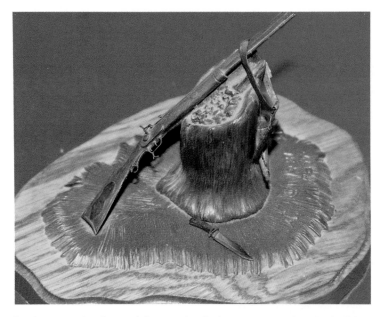

Sculpture of rifle and bowie knife by a stump by Jack Rott. "Montana Jack" Rott was self-taught and his sculptures reflect great detail and understanding. $500.00 – 750.00.

Buffalo Bill Cody mounted on his horse. Made of pot metal and available as souvenirs at the Wild West shows. $75.00 – 135.00.

Plaster poly-chromed bust of Hiawatha. Circa 1900. $95.00 – 225.00.

Las Vegas Hitchhiker. An original wood carving by Gene Zesch. $325.00 – 575.00.

Free Trapper. A life-size bronze of a mountain man by Timothy Rath. One of one. Great execution by a contemporary artist. $5,000.00 +.

Small bronze of a buffalo on a marble base. $375.00 – 500.00.

THE AMERICAN COWBOY —
FREE SPIRIT OF THE RANGE

The American cowboy lived a hard life. Today's "knight of the plains" image is often far from reality. In the outstanding western film *The Culpepper Cattle Company*, there is a scene where the boy who has just joined the trail drive is talking with the cook. The boy has great visions of being a cowboy but has been told he will be the cook's "little Mary." The boy tells the crusty old cook about his dream to become a cowboy. Cookie retorts "Hell kid, a man's a cowboy cause he can't be nothing else." There is a strong measure of truth in that statement. Many cowboys were satisfied with three squares and some cash in their pockets. Cowboys faced hot, stormy, and bone-chilling days as they tended cattle on the ranch or drove them to market.

The cowboy faced a great deal of hardship for what little that most had to show for their efforts after their days on the range were over. On the other hand, he was clearly a free spirit with a full measure of self-esteem and a pronounced knack for enjoying himself. He had great pride is his horsemanship and ability to care for his cattle and, when necessary, his comrades.

Cowboys worked for a small amount of money a month and were able to carry most of their possessions with them. Cowboys were paid $25 to $40 a month and trail bosses made $100 to $150 a month. Sometimes there was a bonus for the trail boss. The lifestyle of a cowboy made it difficult to have a family or possessions. Many of them preferred things that way. The cowboy did, however, take great pride in what he did own. This could include his hat, usually a Stetson, his saddle, chaps and spurs, and a rifle or six-shooter. When a cowpuncher arrived at the end of the trail in towns like Dodge City, Abi-lene, or Ogallala, there was usually a visit to the general store to pick up anything from a new scarf to a fancy Colt's Single Action with carved ivory grips. The stores carried everything to capture the fancy of the cowboy and many of these great items are among today's collectibles.

I have some original photos of cowboys in my collection and the one thing that sets them apart is the individuality expressed in their style of dress. Everything from hats to spurs, chaps to shirts, and belts to boots truly give evidence to the free spirit of the American cowboy.

Cowboys exhibited quite a range in their qualities. They could be caring and very loyal to their outfit and friends. You could trust their word once it was given. Their pleasures were a bit on the wild side but cowboys were products of their times. Enjoyable pastimes included gathering at a saloon, gambling, raising a little hell, admiring the "ladies," talking their own language, eating heartily, telling tall tales and, perhaps most of all, riding the open range.

Cowboy accouterments are today's collectibles. There are many areas. Consider the following: hats, chaps, boots, firearms, whips, shirts, branding irons, ropes and leather lariats, barbed wire, eating utensils, straight razors, saddles, bridles, coats, cuffs, neckerchiefs, knives, diaries, blankets, trail gear, and bunkhouse relics.

Cowboy collectibles are continuing to experience growing interest and prices are reflecting that interest. Specialty antique shows that feature cowboy memorabilia now number over 50 and are growing. Just a few years ago, there were only a handful. As long as the cowboy lives in American history and the legend grows, this trend will continue.

To be a cowboy meant, first of all to be a horseman.
Larry McMurtry, *In a Narrow Grave*, 1978

Photograph of Peter Robidoux's general mercantile store in Wallace, Kansas, circa 1888. It was a favorite place for cowboys to pick up anything from a Colt's six-shooter with carved ivory grips to a straight-razor. $225.00 – 400.00.

Original photo of old-time cowboy. $175.00 – 250.00.

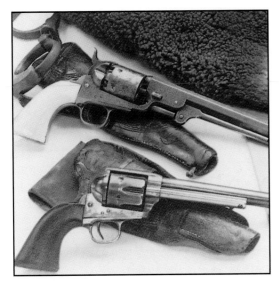

Two firearms favored by cowboys. Top – Colt Model 1851 Navy revolver .36 caliber with ivory grips. $1,700.00 – 3,500.00. Colt Single Action Army with walnut grips, 7½" barrel, .45 caliber, nickel-plated. $1,700.00 – 4,000.00.

Pepper box. $450.00 – 1,100.00.

Matched set of stamped holsters and belt for Colt Single Action Army. The maker is A.W. Brill, Austin, Texas. Near mint condition. $375.00 – 650.00.

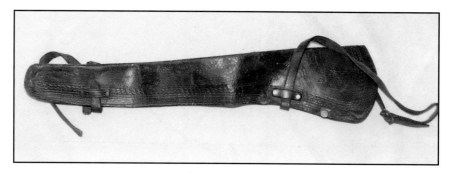

A Winchester rifle scabbard. Rifles were often carried by cowboys because they were more accurate and not as cumbersome as pistols. $125.00 – 250.00.

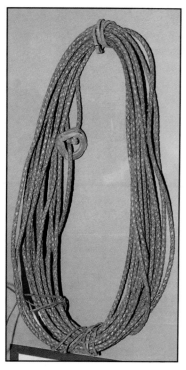

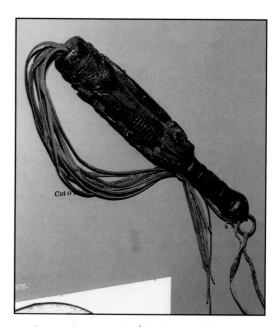

A cat o' nine tails. $275.00 – 350.00.

Braided rawhide rope. $175.00 – 400.00.

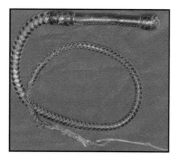

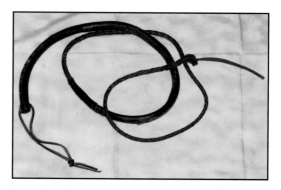

Long leather bull whip, circa 1880. $225.00 – 350.00.

A short bull whip. $175.00 – 250.00.

⌣: ✣ ✣ :⌣

You never saw an old cowpuncher. They were scarce as hen's teeth. Where they went to, heaven only knows.

⌣: John Clay – *My Life on the Range* :⌣

A bearskin coat that found favor during the harsh winters on the plains. $350.00 – 525.00.

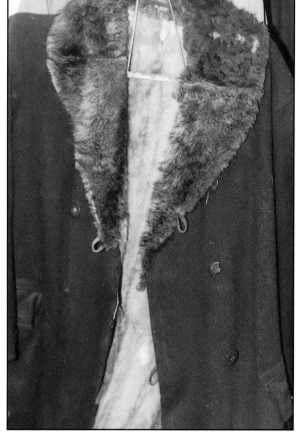

A heavy and warm cowboy coat with a buffalo-trimmed collar. $375.00 – 650.00.

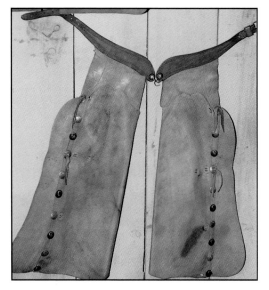

A pair of chaps with 20 silver conchos. $425.00 – 650.00.

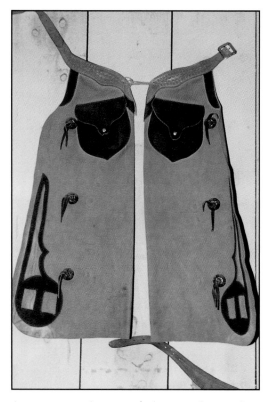

A custom-made pair of chaps with six silver conchos. $425.00 – 650.00.

Wooly chaps in fine overall condition. $725.00 – 1,250.00.

A fine pair of leather chaps with two pockets and silver conchos. Referred to as batwing chaps. $425.00 – 650.00.

Decorated cowboy cuff with studded star design. $125.00 – 225.00 for the pair.

Two sets of cowboy cuffs. One is for special use only, such as parades. The other set was used by a working cowboy. It has a studded design featuring stars. $175.00 – 350.00 per set.

Original photo of three Colorado cowboys. It appears one has started to celebrate early (for the benefit of the camera) and the one on the right has his rifle ready for action. $175.00 – 275.00.

A great set of custom spurs with an embossed eagle and the owner's initials. Tooled leather straps. $325.00 – 600.00.

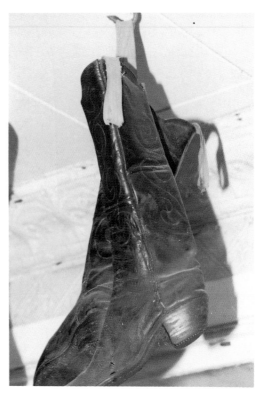

Cowboy boots, circa 1880. $225.00 – 475.00.

120

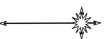
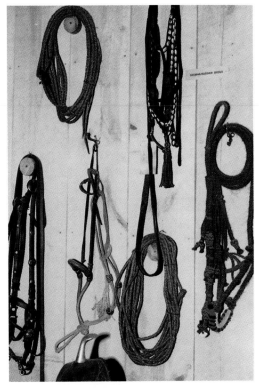

A variety of braided lariats and bridles. $175.00 – 400.00 each.

A grouping of braided lariats and bridles. $175.00 – 400.00 each.

The American Cowboy is one of the few national legends to have become a myth while he is still a fact...

◡ Daniel Boorstin, *The American Cowboy* ◠

Large branding iron. $125.00 – 250.00.

A great variety of branding irons. $55.00 – 250.00 each.

Texas steer dehorner. This has a five-inch throat to accommodate the large horns. $350.00 – 575.00.

A variety of barbed wire samples. This was the nemesis of the cowboy until it became necessary to use it on cattle ranches. "String wire" was not a favored duty. $8.00 – 45.00 for a short strand depending on scarcity. Some very rare specimens can command an even higher price.

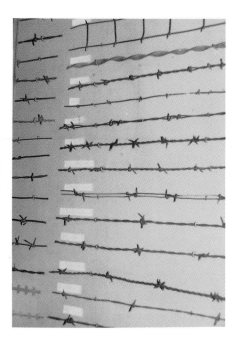

(Cowboys)...as a class, they are foul-mouthed, drunken, lecherous, utterly corrupt. Usually harmless on the plains when sober, they are dreaded in the towns, for then liquor has ascendency over them.

✧ Frank Leslie's *Illustrated Weekly*, Jan. 14, 1882 ✧

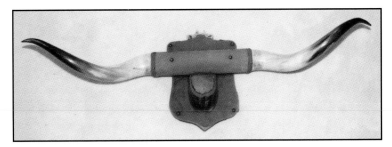

Mounted longhorns, circa 1890. $275.00 – 425.00.

An unusual double-horned wall rack. $400.00 – 600.00.

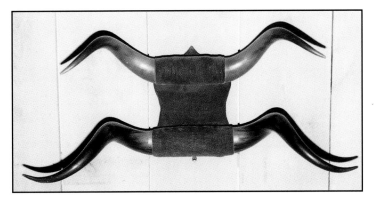

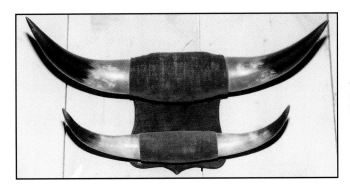

An early pair of mounted bull horns. These could often be found in the ranchhoue or bunkhouse. $175.00 – 300.00.

Large pair of mounted Texas longhorns with leather binding. $325.00 – 550.00.

A horn rack made in the form of a horseshoe. $250.00 – 375.00.

Mounted long horn steer. $525.00 – 900.00.

Barber chair from Kansas. This chair had many cowboy customers during their visits to town. $450.00 – 750.00.

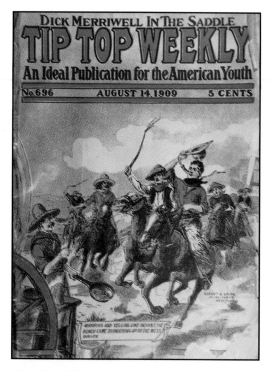

Tip Top Weekly published in 1909 for 5 cents. The caption reads "Whooping and yelling like Indians, the bunch came thundering up to the mess wagon." $12.00 – 25.00.

When it came time for that occasional Saturday-night bath at the bunkhouse, tubs similar to this one were often used. $135.00 – 175.00.

Early examples of straight razors. $32.00 – 45.00 each.

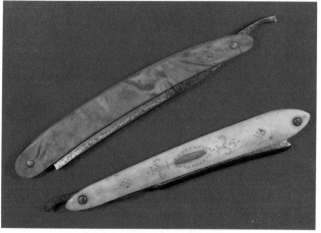

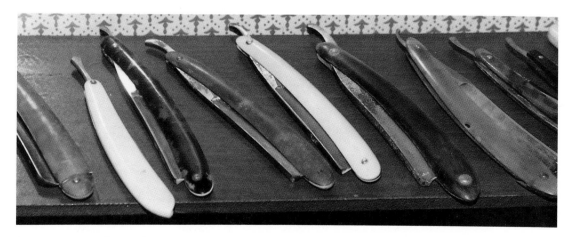

A nice variety of straight razors. The cowboy had one available at the bunkhouse and would frequently, if on the move, carry one in his saddlebags. $12.00 – 35.00.

Binoculars for saddlebags. Used on a cattle ranch in Texas. Brass frames. $225.00 – 325.00.

Wooden bootjack that was in frequent use around the bunkhouse. $35.00 – 65.00.

A couple of wool blankets of the type that were favored by cowboys. $135.00 – 250.00.

SADDLES & SPURS

The major source of transportation on the Western Frontier was horseback. Well-made saddles were a necessity. They were expensive to purchase and generally received special care. Saddlemakers were proud of their craftmenship and such names as Frazier, Miles City Saddlery Co., and Meanea were eagerly purchased and remain favorites among today's collectors.

Some of the early saddle shops were one-man operations while others became quite large with many employees. Shops were located throughout the West, with many in Texas. Saddles had to accomodate the heavy work of roping, bronco busting, and other tasks around the ranch. Selecting a saddle was a personal matter and in addition to the fundamental qualities; style, hand-carving, and ornamentation were all very important. A cowboy considered his saddle a friend and used it for a back support around the campfire as well as a rest for sleeping. As a testament to the care given to saddles, I have seen examples that were made prior to 1900 that continue to appear in outstanding condition. Cowboys and others in the Old West were frequently judged by the quality and condition of their saddle and a fine one was a great source of pride.

Collectors favor saddles that were made prior to 1900 which include the maker's name. Many were made without a name. Placing an approximate date of manufacture on a saddle can be very difficult. The overall styles of saddles have not changed and, in many instances, there are old-style models available on the market that may have been made just last year.

Saddles with extensive decorations and markings are very desirable. Handcarving along with silver, conchos, and brass studs offer a lot to the character of a saddle. Unless money is no object, I would recommend that the collector seek to purchase just one saddle but make certain it is of the finest quality and vintage that you can afford. It should always prove to be a wise investment.

Another very personal item among cowboys and others were spurs. Spurs are attracting a great deal of collector interest and prices continue to escalate. I have seen so many examples that it is easy to conclude that there were about as many different styles as cowboys. The designs range from a basic utility-type spur to those that were made with great care and personalized with silver and even gold.

Most cowboys preferred large-rowled spurs because they had more points and did not injure the horse flanks if used properly. Riders in the Old West valued their horses and cruelty with spurs was uncommon.

There was a time not too many years ago that the collector could find a saddle or a set of spurs and assume that the items were what they appeared to be. Prices were generally low and there was no reason to add "history" to those collectibles. In today's market, however, the collector must be alert to altered items. This can include adding bogus makers' marks, restoration that diminishes value, and misrepresentation. As always, it is wise to learn as much as possible and deal with reputable people. With enough exposure, the collector will soon develop an ability to make good purchases. The booming interest in saddles and spurs has created a need to purchase with wisdom and a healthy dose of caution.

Saddle up and hit the trail.

A Western cliche

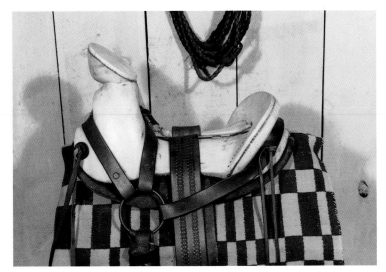

Spanish saddle. One of the forerunners of the cowboy saddle. $550.00 – 825.00.

This saddle has seen a great deal of use. It would make a nice relic. $65.00 – 125.00.

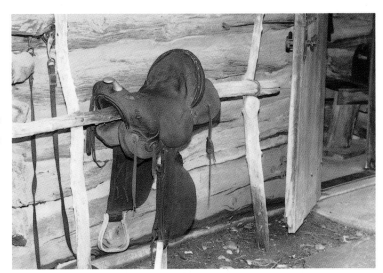

Typical ranch saddle. $325.00 – 475.00.

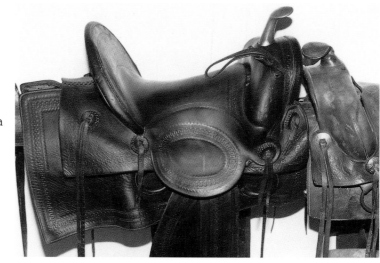

A durable black leather saddle with a stamped design. $450.00 – 625.00.

Custom saddle. $750.00 – 1,200.00.

Well-made California-style saddle, leather, wood, and metal. Basket-stamped and carved with matching saddle bags. $1,500.00 – 2,250.00.

Elaborately carved California-style saddle in outstanding condition. $2,100.00 – 3,400.00.

Fine quality stamped leather and decorated parade saddle. Extensive silver work. $3,500.00 – 6,500.00.

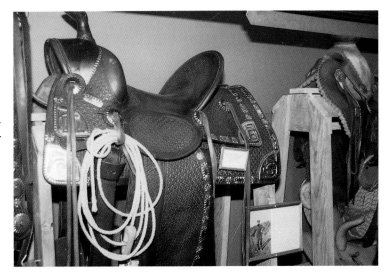

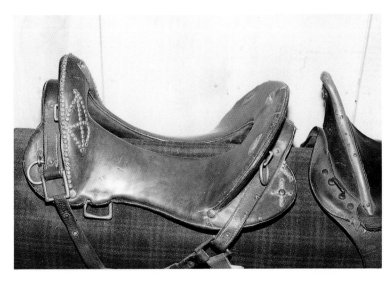

Military saddle with brass studs. $250.00 – 475.00.

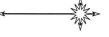
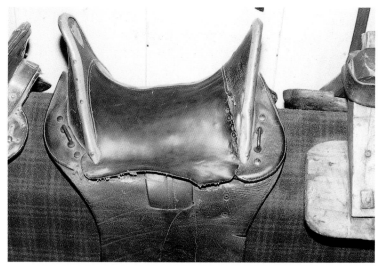

Military leather saddle with brass trim. $525.00 – 725.00.

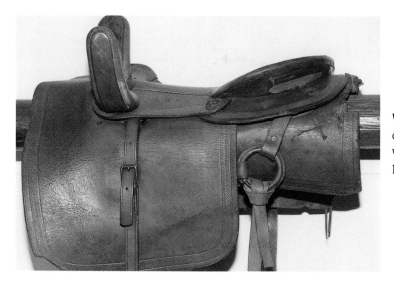

Woman's sidesaddle. These were frequently used in the Old West but they were not comfortable or particularly practical. $375.00 – 550.00.

Woman's sidesaddle. Contrasting leather. $275.00 – 500.00.

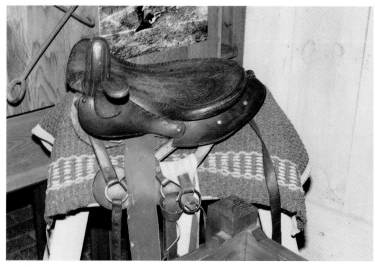

Woman's sidesaddle. Floral fabric design with leather. $450.00 – 750.00.

Woman's sidesaddle. Hand-carved star design. $450.00 – 750.00.

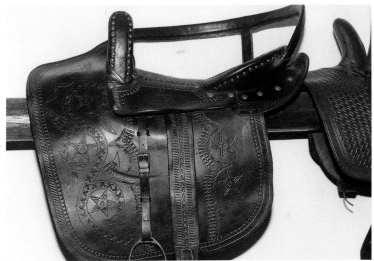

A fine western saddle with large skirts. $850.00 – 1,750.00.

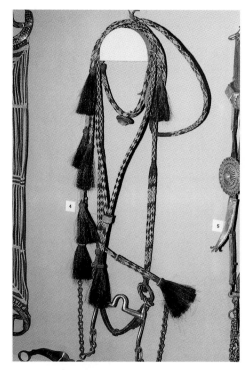

Braided horsehair bridle, circa 1900.
$425.00 – 675.00.

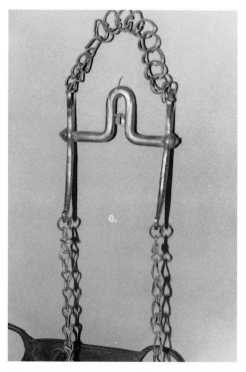

A basic port-mouth bit. $40.00 – 65.00.

Unusual early bridle and bit. Hand-forged
bit. $250.00 – 400.00.

Steel military bit. $85.00 – 135.00.

Spade bit. $225.00 – 350.00.

Jointed-mouth bit with twist. $15.00 – 25.00.

An unusual amount of horse stealing has been carried on of late.... A few wholesome hangings will soon be in order, and the traffic in horseflesh will be sensibly diminished. We advise these jailbirds to make themselves scarce in this section if they don't want to pull hemp.

☙ Fort Worth Democrat – May 1874 ❧

Early hand-forged bit. $75.00 – 135.00.

Hurry it up. I'm due in Hell for dinner.

☙ Black Jack Ketchum to the hangman ❧

Quality silver bit. $675.00 – 800.00.

Silver on brass California-type bit.
$950.00 – 1250.00.

A highly decorated bridle and bit consisting of silver
and turquoise. $1,350.00 – 2,750.00.

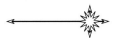

The finest lad I ever met.

∽ John Tunstall on Billy the Kid ∾

Silver and turquoise bridle and bit. Includes silver buckles. Elaborate design. $1,850.00 – 3,600.00.

Wooden stirrups. $45.00 – 75.00 per pair.

A variety of wooden stirrups. $45.00 – 75.00 per pair.

Brass spurs with original straps.
$150.00 – 275.00.

Steel spurs with original leather straps.
$185.00 – 375.00.

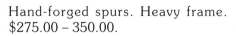

Hand-forged spurs. Heavy frame.
$275.00 – 350.00.

A pair of well-made spurs with silver conchas on the leathers. $375.00 – 625.00.

A beautiful pair of silver inlaid Charro-type spurs. $375.00 – 700.00.

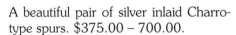

Spurs, early steel without leathers. $225.00 – 350.00.

Double-mounted silver inlay spurs in fine condition. $375.00 – 450.00.

Southwestern style spurs with Mexican style rowels. $265.00 – 450.00.

Spurs with large rowels. Original leather straps. $225.00 – 425.00.

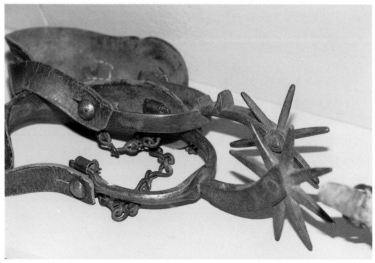

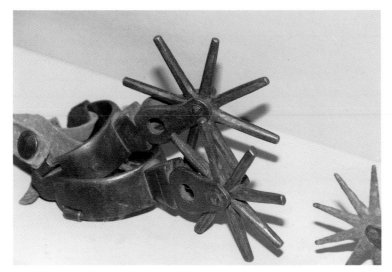

Mexican spurs with large, blunt rowels. $175.00 – 325.00.

Double-mounted silver inlay spurs with stamped leathers. Fine condition. $525.00 – 750.00.

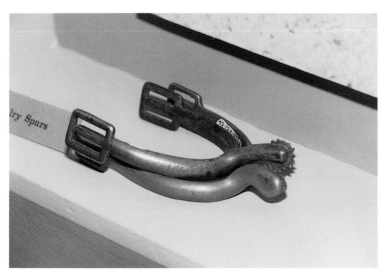

Cavalry spurs. $85.00 – 135.00.

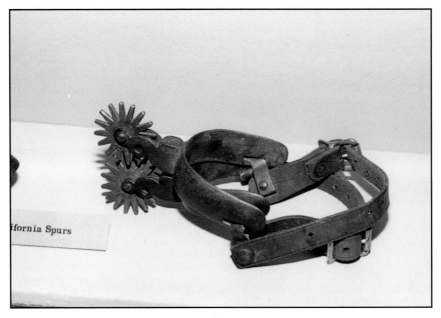

California spurs. $175.00 – 350.00.

California spurs. Replaced leather. $175.00 – 300.00 for a set.

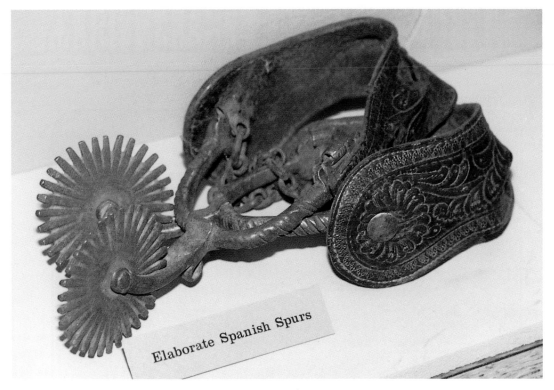

Elaborate Spanish spurs. $235.00 – 475.00.

NICKNAMES

Poker Alice – Alice Tubbs (1851 – 1930) mining town gambler.

Texas Jack – John Burwell Omohundro (1846 – 1880) Western scout, actor, and member of Buffalo Bill's Wild West Show.

Johnny-Behind-The-Duece – John O'Rourke, Tombstone gambler.

Cattle Kate – Ella Watson (1862 – 1889) lynched in Wyoming, accused of rustling.

Soapy Smith – Jefferson Smith (1860 – 1898) saloon owner and confidence man. Shot and killed during the Alaska gold rush.

NATIVE AMERICAN COLLECTIBLES

 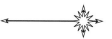
Recent years have witnessed a tremendous amount of interest in the American Indian culture. The history of our Native Americans is fascinating and offers numerous lessons for contemporary society. Before the closing of the frontier, there were collectors of Indian artifacts. Many friendships developed between Indian people and whites which resulted in the giving of gifts. Other items were purchased or traded for. Many of the early artists of the Old West insisted on historical accuracy and felt it was necessary to have Native Indian artifacts in their studios for reference.

When one takes a look at Hollywood's treatment and depiction of the American Indian, we have witnessed a real evolution. Gone are the days of white actors dressing up and portraying the Indian with questionable costuming and props. We now have films like *Dances with Wolves* that bring the Indian people to the screen with true feeling and understanding. Books like *500 Nations — An Illustrated History of North American Indians* by Alvin M. Josephy, Jr. and *A Pictorial History of the American Indian* by Oliver LaFarge have made major contributions to the understanding and appreciation of this wonderful culture.

Today's collector can seek out early items as well as the great craftmanship of modern collectibles including blankets, bead work, silversmithing, art work, and other native crafts.

To aid the collector in the understanding of the American Indian and his artifacts, it is helpful to possess as much understanding as possible. To that purpose, I will define some major areas of interest.

Beads – Beads were made of numerous materials including shells, wood, teeth, claws, seeds, clay, bird beaks, bone, and minerals. Glass beads were brought by the settlers and formed a big item of trade.

Sinew – This is a part of the animal known as the tendon. It was taken from along the backbone of the deer, bison, or other large animal. It is pounded and dried for use in sewing. Fishing lines and ropes were made from braided or twisted sinew.

Parfleche – This is a tough bag or box made from rawhide with the hair removed. It is usually painted or decorated and used to carry a variety of items. Made primarily by the Plains Indians and those in the Rocky Mountain region.

Axes – Indian axes vary in size from a few ounces to 30 pounds. Usually they are from one to six pounds. In general, the ax is rather heavy and wedge shaped. They were usually made from granite or other hard rock, although sandstones and slates were used when harder material was not available. One groove was usually curved around the thick part of the ax. The shaft was usually fastened with sinew or rawhide. The ax was used for many things, including warfare. Iron axes brought by whites were much sought after by the Indians.

Moccasins – The Western or Plains tribes wore a moccasin with a hard sole and a soft upper. The shapes and designs and the materials used in making the moccasins vary from tribe to tribe. This was influenced by the type of country lived in and the animals available for use. Dyes from plants such as roots, berries, and leaves were used for designs as well as porcupine quills and later on, beads, shells, and buttons. The design sometimes had a symbolism and the colors used also had a special meaning. Some moccasins were used for special ceremonies. Deer skin was the most generally used skin.

Dyes – Indian dyes were made of many materials. The materials to be dyed and the materials at hand decided what colors would be used. Lichens, roots, berries, pokeberries, bloodroot, sumac, grapes, alder, and other materials were used.

Flint – A variety of chalcedony. Used by the Indians for making a number of implements such as arrowheads, spearheads, knives, and scrapers.

Arrow – The Indian arrow had six parts: the head, shaft, foreshaft, shaftment, the

 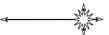

feathering, and the nock. The head was the point of the arrow. The shaft was the main, rod-like part, which sometimes had a piece of a harder material attached to it at the front end, called the foreshaft. The shaftment was the other end of the shaft, and the nock, the end which grooved the bowstring. The feathering was the feathers attached at the end. Usually the shaft was plain. The Plains Indians cut grooves lengthwise which were sometimes called "lightening marks" or "blood grooves." Some arrows had no feathers; others had either two or three feathers. The feathers were from a great variety of birds.

Authentic Native American collectibles are becoming scarce and the best sources are reliable dealers and auction houses. There remain, however, many finds just waiting for the astute collector. Antique shops in general will occasionally have an item or two for sale. Trading with other collectors is another good source. A word of caution is in order. Indian artifacts are frequently reproduced and touched up. It is wise to read as much as possible on the subject, visit museums, view private collections whenever possible, and talk with knowledgeable collectors and other experts.

✧✧

Navajos have fine flocks of sheep, abundance of mules and herds of cattle of a superior kind. They have gardens and peach orchards. Several articles of their woolen manufacture equal the quality of ours.

Samuel Patton, 1824, first American report on the Navajo

Original photograph of a Sioux warrior, circa 1880. $250.00 – 375.00.

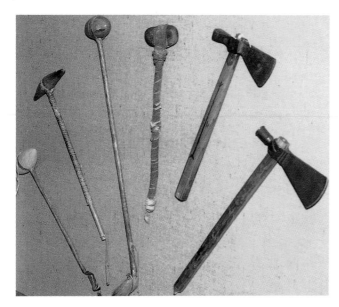

Left to right: Plains Indian stone-headed war club. $225.00 – 350.00. Western Plains Indian war club. $175.00 – 250.00. War club, rawhide wrapped stone with horsehair drop. $300.00 – 425.00. Another stone-headed club with rawhide wrap. $175.00 – 250.00. Plains tomahawk. $450.00 – 600.00. Hudson Bay-style pipe tomahawk. $525.00 – 775.00.

Rawhide-covered saddle with stirrups. Plains Indian. Scarce. $750.00 – 1,350.00.

Rawhide-covered saddle with stirrups. Plains Indian. Difficult to find in this condition. $825.00 – 1,500.00.

I claim a right to live on my land, and accord you the privilege to live on yours.

⤳ Chief Joseph ⤶

An overall scene of Plains Indian quivers and saddles. The other item is a parleche, or container, in rawhide with painted design.

Decorated parfleche or container in rawhide. Northern Plains Indian. $375.00 – 625.00.

Decorated elk-skin quiver with arrows. Quiver, $575.00 – 750.00. Arrows, $135.00 – 225.00 each.

 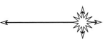

Typical Plains Indian dress. Buckskin-beaded shirt. $625.00 – 850.00. Pants. $300.00 – 450.00. Magnificent war bonnet. $950.00 – 1,500.00.

⁂

If I were an Indian, I think that I would greatly prefer to cast my lot among those of my people who adhered to the free open plains, rather than submit to the quiet, unexciting, uneventful life of a reservation.

∽ General George Armstrong Custer ∽

American Plains Indian large drums. Stretched rawhide. Left, $375.00 – 550.00. Right with painted design, $450.00 – 875.00.

Top left – American Western Plains Indian tom tom painted design on rawhide. $275.00 – 500.00. Plains rifle. $700.00 – 1,325.00. No rawhide or brass exhibited.

American Western Plains Indian tom tom. Entirely covered on both sides with rawhide. Original painted decoration on both sides. Very good condition. $225.00 – 450.00.

American Western Indian roach or headpiece. Late nineteenth century. Worn as an ornament in the center of a shaved head. $325.00 – 550.00.

Copyrighted, 1882, by Bailey, Dix & Mead.

Original photograph of One Bull. He was a nephew of Sitting Bull and a skillful warrior. Copyrighted 1882, by Bailey, Dix and Mead. Cabinet size. $250.00 – 375.00.

✦✦

Man for man an Injun's as good as a white man any day. When he's a good friend, he's the best friend in the world.

✦ Charles M. Russell ✦

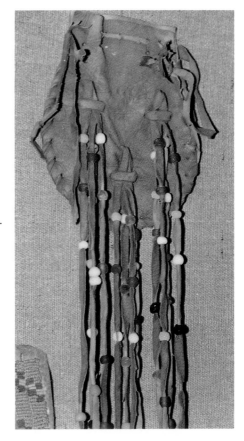

Western Plains Indian possibles bag with beads. $375.00 – 525.00.

✦✦

The Indians will sometimes, when in mourning or on other solemn occassions, give away the whole of their possessions.

✦ Francis Parkman, *The Oregon Trail* ✦

 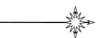

Plains Indian leather beaded pipe bag. $950.00 – 1,300.00.

Souix pipe bag with beadwork and quill trim. $950.00 – 1,650.00. Wampum pouch. $225.00 – 375.00. Beaded knife sheath. $325.00 – 450.00.

Plains Indian beaded pipe bag. $950.00 – 1400.00. Beaded belts, elaborate designs. $250.00 – 325.00 each.

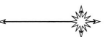

Western Plains Indian beaded buckskin moccasins. $325.00 – 450.00.

Western Plains Indian beaded buckskin moccasins. Tops entirely covered. $325.00 – 450.00.

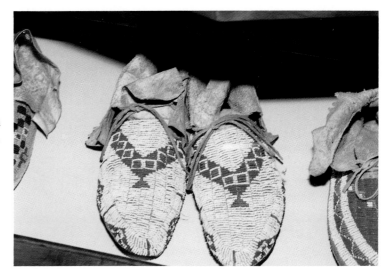

Western Plains Indian beaded buckskin moccasins. $300.00 – 425.00.

A pair of Western Plains Indian beaded buckskin moccasins. Fine detailed beadwork. $450.00 – 700.00.

Western Plains Indian beaded buckskin moccasins. Large pair, $275.00 – 425.00. Small pair, $225.00 – 325.00.

Western Plains Indian beaded buckskin moccasins. Tops almost entirely covered. $450.00 – 750.00.

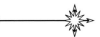

Plains Indian beaded buckskin moccasins. Extensive coverage. Very attractive design. $450.00 – 750.00.

Western Plains Indian beaded buckskin moccasins. $225.00 – 450.00.

Western Plains Indian beaded buckskin moccasins. Limited bead work. $175.00 – 225.00.

Plains Indian beaded pipe bag with floral design. $750.00 – 950.00.

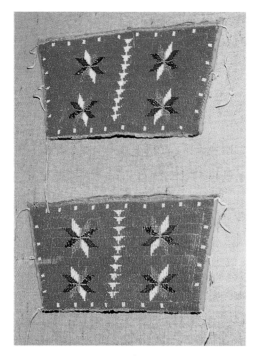

Beaded armbands. $275.00 – 400.00 per pair.

Native American Indian beaded panels. Center, $950.00 – 1,250.00. Right, $425.00 – 600.00.

Pair of fringed and beaded gauntlets. $275.00 – 450.00.

That is how Indians learn to do things. We watch the old people when we are young.

Berina Cordero, Cochiti Pueblo

Cigar store Indian. This one has been restored and repainted, circa 1885. $7,500.00 – 13,500.00.

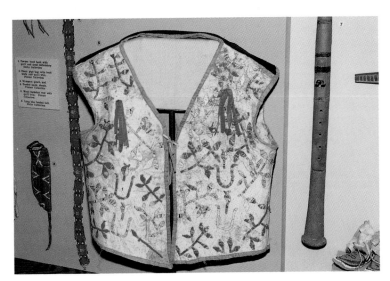

Elaborate beaded vest. $475.00 – 825.00.

A ROUNDUP OF WESTERN COLLECTIBLES — CLOSING THOUGHTS

 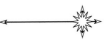

It is my feeling that interest in our frontier heritage will continue to flourish and grow. It is perplexing to note, however, that interest in Western memorabilia is a fairly recent phenomenon. Yes, there have been collectors of early firearms for decades but where were the chaps, spurs, and relic collectors? They have now emerged with a bang and their numbers continue to grow daily. Specialty shows with an Old West theme are expanding and significant historical documents are bringing unheard of prices.

The continuing escalation of prices is something to behold! Where will this trend lead us? My personal feeling is that some of the reported auction prices are unrealistic and it is questionable that the market will sustain some of these levels. Collectors of antique firearms can attest that the market was very hot several years back but the cooling off period did arrive and many sales were at less than the original purchase price. Another example is in the area of antique advertising. A few years ago, an item brought about $90,000 at auction. The same item recently brought about half of that figure. My intention is not to create concern and apprehension among collectors. I feel the the first rule is to purchase an item if you truly are excited by it and feel you need to own it. It follows that you will have a great deal of enjoyment from your purchase and if the market should go down as a result of waning interest and high prices, you still have your collectible to enjoy.

As a devoted collector, I'm the first to admit that I have clearly paid too much for a piece from time to time. We all have. Fine collectibles are in short supply and are only available when you find them. Many of us have witnessed two individuals at a show discovering a great item at about the same time. While one contemplates the purchase, the other takes possession and makes the purchase. How disappointing! It seems like that item substantially grows in desirability once it is in the hands of another collector.

On the plus side, I feel that the collector of Western Americana has the very best of two worlds. With the fairly recent growth in the collector's market, new discoveries are being made daily. There is also a growing number of specialty businesses that can provide the enthusiast with historically accurate clothing, hats, boots, and leather goods. Many of these dealers are also collectors and have considerable pride in the authenticity and quality of their goods. Some of the companies that I can heartily endorse are Red River of Tujunga, California; River Junction Trade Company of McGregor, Iowa; Old West Reproductions of Florence, Montanta; Trail's End of Erie, Kansas; and Cedar Ridge Clothing Company of Verdugo City, California. These companies have catalogs available and are fine people to deal with. I know that there are others but I'm not familiar with them. For the collector interested in authentic goods, it can be very satisfying to discover a new source. These businesses can range from a one-person operation to a company with several employees. They all have one thing in common — a true love of the Old West.

I have made an effort in this book to illustrate a wide variety of collectibles and concentrate on items that have not been generally illustrated in other books. I did not include a large section on firearms or gunleather because I feel these subjects have had ample coverage in specialty books. On the subject of gunleather, I strongly endorse *Packing Iron — Gunleather of the Frontier West* by Richard C. Rattenbury. I can not imagine a better book on the subject.

My prices reflect a range because I have witnessed sales that fall within a range. We all hope to pay as little as possible but that is not often possible. One dealer or individual's price can be in the lower or higher range or, as we all know, the asking price can frequently exceed what appears to be logic and reason. In that case, the collector must employ his or her best negotiating skills and hope there is

room for compromise. If not, one is confronted with a very serious decision to make. In that regard, it has been my experience that remorse is more often a factor in what was not purchased when the opportunity was present. The potential acquisition of a desirable Western collectible can be one of the most fulfilling moments in the collecting process, even rivaling actual ownership.

I made mention of the situation regarding antique firearms several years back. That situation has changed again. Some feel that Hollywood's new enthusiasm for the Western film has fanned the flames of renewed interest in firearms of the Civil War and Frontier West. As we know, many of the weapons used in the Civil War went West when hostilities ceased and great interest in the American West developed. One dealer advises that the prices of Henry rifles have increased 50% in the last several years. There has been a notable rise in demand and prices for fine firearms with a Western heritage.

Chapter one of this book is devoted to the role of Hollywood in sparking interest in the Old West. I continue to feel that Hollywood's impact can not be discounted. A film like *Dances with Wolves* can reach millions of people and create a lasting impact. Hollywood has the opportunity to explore the telling of many stories and do so with a measure of historical correction and accuracy. Mythic settings will still remain but there is a creative opportunity to provide more than a morality play. I have had the opportunity to be on some movie sets and it is truly exciting to see the attention paid to that true hardscrabble look and authenticity. The recent PBS specials on the Old West have made a great contribution to our understanding of America's frontier history. They have also provided additional enthusiasm among collectors.

My hat's off to collectors. Through their interest, they are preserving a great deal of heritage and adding to our body of knowledge. I know that Hollywood has utilized some long-time collectors as consultants which can certainly serve to enhance the final product.

I can recall walking on the main street of the ghost town of Tincup, Colorado, several years ago. The sun was fading from the sky and the tall pines were growing black. At that elevation, the breeze was becoming cool. There was no other person present. I could visualize what the old mining camp must have been like in its heyday. My walk was in two worlds but, for several moments, I was captivated by the feeling that it was suddenly 1870s' boom times and I was heading for a saloon. You could almost hear the old-time piano and happy voices. It sure made my spirit soar!

My wish is that all of my readers strike pay dirt in their collectibles search as well as a square deal! Keep prospecting, but watch that trail.

Taken from County Jail and lynched by Bisbee mob in Tombstone, Feb. 22nd, 1884

John Heath, Boothill Cemetary, Tombstone

Adams Express strongbox with original green paint. $2,250.00 – 3,750.00.

Adams Express Company office sign. Embossed, heavy paper. $175.00 – 350.00.

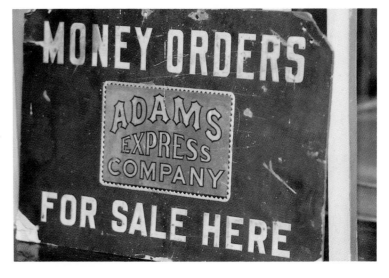

Western sheriff's office, circa 1900. Oak rolltop desk. $1,750.00 – 3,200.00. Oak-cased telephone. $225.00 – 375.00. Club. $85.00 – 165.00. Lantern. $75.00 – 110.00. Kerosene lamp. $55.00 – 85.00. Large wall clock. $475.00 – 850.00. Handcuffs. $45.00 – 75.00. Union Leader tobacco tin. $35.00 – 55.00.

Portable jail cell. Frequently seen in frontier town. $3,500.00 plus.

Grizzly bear rug, circa 1900. $550.00 – 750.00.

I was considered the most reckless and daring rider and one of the best shots in the western country.

∽ Calamity Jane ∽

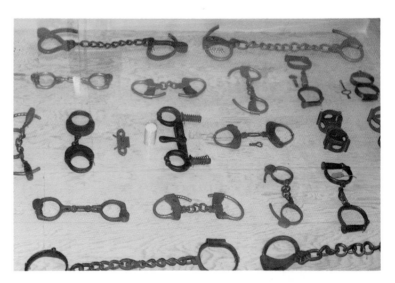

A variety of handcuffs and restraining devices used by lawmen of the Old West. $50.00 – 450.00 each.

Mounted buffalo head. A large bull. $750.00 – 1,250.00.

Kickapoo Indian Salve sign on canvass. $2,500.00 – 5,000.00.

Wells Fargo & Co. express box. $1,800.00 – 3,500.00.

 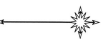

Guns often seen in the Old West. From top to bottom: 1858 Remington Percussion revolver, .44 caliber. $550.00 – 1,250.00. 1858 Remington Percussion revolver, .36 caliber. $600.00 – 2,000.00. Merwin & Hulbert revolver, 1876 Army model, .44 caliber. $550.00 – 1,250.00. 1895 Colt revolver, New Army model, .38 caliber. $275.00 – 700.00. Belgian Army revolver imported 1880 – 1884 as competition to the Colt. Fired Winchester 44-40 cartridges. $225.00 – 375.00.

The value of a specific firearm can vary substantially. Value is based on scarcity, condition, demand, and original parts. For example, a common model Colt Percussion, model 1860, in poor condition can bring as little as a few hundred dollars. The same model in "near mint" condition, with all original parts and grips, could bring several thousand dollars.

Favored guns of the Western frontier. From top to bottom: Colt Percussion revolver, Army model 1860. $650.00 – 5,000.00. This firearm could be equipped with a detachable shoulder stock. Colt Percussion revolver, Navy model 1861, .36 caliber. $725.00 – 5,500.00. Manhatten percussion revolver, .36 caliber. $300.00 – 725.00. Colt Percussion revolver, model 1849, .31 caliber, bottom two. $425.00 – 1,050.00.

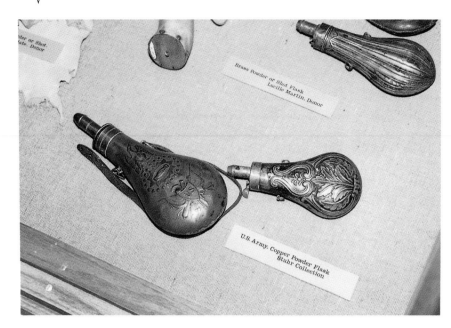

Left – U.S. Army copper powder flask. Right and above right – two brass powder or shot flasks. $95.00 – 225.00 each.

Elk ink stand with bottle. $75.00 – 115.00.

I sincerely believe that there were not less than 10,000 buffalo within a circle of two miles.

∿ Captain Meriwether Lewis, near Great Falls, Montana, 1806 ∿

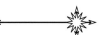

Original painting by Ron Stewart entitled *Man of Nature.* $225.00 – 350.00.

Large lithograph of a cowgirl equipped with a whip and a six gun, circa 1900. $375.00 – 600.00.

Wooden match holder given out with the compliments of W.A. Speer, Hardware & Furniture, Clements, Kansas. $24.00 – 35.00.

Massive Bowie knife with bone handle and brass backstrap. Heavy leather scabbard. Made by the famous Montana knifemaker, Rudolph Ruana. $475.00 – 650.00.

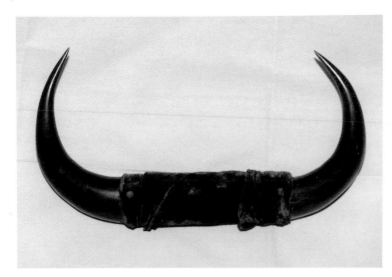

Buffalo horns covered with blue fabric. $45.00 – 60.00.

Elk saloon tray. O.F.C. Bourbon, The George T. Stagg Company. $85.00 – 135.00.

Wooden cigar store Indian, circa 1890. $7,500.00 – 15,000.00 and up. Value is influenced by scarcity, condition, and uniqueness.

✧✦✦✧

Once I moved about like the wind. Now I surrender to you and that is all.

Geronimo to General Crook, 1866

Buckingham Bright Cut Plug Smoking Tobacco pocket tin. Great color & graphics. $25.00 – 75.00.

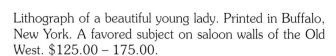

Lithograph of a beautiful young lady. Printed in Buffalo, New York. A favored subject on saloon walls of the Old West. $125.00 – 175.00.

Cabinet photo of two subjects displaying their weapons. Taken in Oregon. $225.00 – 375.00.

Mounted moose head. $325.00 – 550.00.

Mounted elk head. $250.00 – 400.00.

Early framed print entitled *At Noon Time* depicts cattle. Very unique with horns mounted to the frame. From a Wyoming ranch house. $375.00 – 450.00.

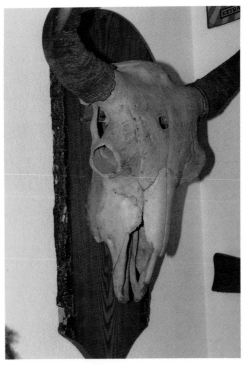

Large buffalo skull mounted on a large piece of redwood. $325.00 – 450.00.

An unusual child's chair constructed of goat horns and hide. This one came from a Montana ranch house. $525.00 – 800.00.

This type of regulator clock was seen throughout the American frontier in express offices, saloons, general stores, hotels, and barber shops. $450.00 – 600.00.

Pony Express saddle. Very rare.

Adams, Ramon. *The Old-Time Cowhand*. New York: The Macmillan Company, 1961.

Ainsworth, Ed. *The Cowboy in Art*. Cleveland, Ohio: The World Publishing Co.,1968.

Anderson, Warren R. *Owning Western History — A Guide to Collecting*. Missoula, Montana: Mountain Press Publishing Co., 1993.

Berkebile, Don H. *American Carriages, Sleighs, Sulkies and Carts*. New York: Dover Publications, Inc., 1977.

Billington, Ray Allen. *Westward Expansion — A History of the American Frontier*. New York: The Macmillan Company, 1960.

Cromie, Alice. *Tour Guide to the Old West*. New York: Times Books, 1977.

Davis, Marvin & Helen. *Relics of the Whiteman*. Ashland, Oregon: Winema Publications, 1973.

Davis, William C. *The American Frontier — Pioneers, Settlers & Cowboys*. New York: Smithmark, 1992.

Drache, Hiram M. *The Challenge of the Prairie*. Minneapolis, Minnesota: The Lund Press, 1970.

Erdoes, Richard. *Saloons of the Old West*. New York: Alfred A. Knopf, 1979.

Foster, Harrid. *The Look of the Old West*. New York: Viking Press, 1955.

Heide, Robert, and John Gilman. *Cowboy Collectibles*. New York: Harper & Row, 1982.

Hoffman, Wilber. *Sagas of Old Western Travel & Transport*. San Diego, California: Howell North Publishers, Inc., 1980.

Hamma, Elizabeth. *Stagecoach Days*. Menlo Park, California: Lane Books, 1975.

Kennedy, Michael S. *Cowboys and Cattlemen*. New York: Hastings House Publishers. 1964.

Knowles, Thomas W. and Joe R. Lansdale. *Wild West Show!* New York: Random House, 1994

Lamar, Howard R. *The Reader's Encyclopedia of the American West*. New York: Thomas Y. Crowell Company, 1977.

Lawliss, Chuck. *Ghost Towns, Gamblers & Gold*. New York: Gallery Books, 1985.

LaFarge, Oliver. *A Pictorial History of the American Indian.* New York: Crown Publishers, 1957.

Marks, Paula Mitchell. *Precious Dust — The American Gold Rush Era: 1848 – 1900.* New York: William Morrow and Company, Inc., 1994.

National Park Service. *Prospector, Cowhand and Sodbuster.* Washington, D.C.: United States Department of the Interior, 1967.

Reader's Digest. *Story of the Great American West.* Pleasantville, New York: The Reader's Digest Association, Inc., 1967.

Sennett, Ted. *Great Hollywood Westerns.* New York: Harry N. Abrams, Inc., Publishers, 1990.

Warner Books. The Wild West. New York: Time-Life Books, 1993.

Weis, Norman D. *Helldorados — Ghosts and Camps of the Old Southwest.* Caldwell, Idaho: The Caxton Printers, Ltd., 1977.

Wilson, Rufus Rockwell. *Out of the West.* New York: The Press of the Pioneers, 1933.

During my travels throughout the American West over a thirty year period, I have had the wonderful opportunity to visit museums and historical sites in the Old West. Some were small county museums and others were major displays developed by private individuals and government. To come up with a list of my top thirty was a bit difficult. There are many that I remember fondly, both in terms of their great collections and the friendliness of the staff.

My list is in no particular order. Whenever the opportunity permits, I would strongly recommend visits to all of them. The collector of Western Americana will be very rewarded!

ARIZONA
Tombstone, Arizona
Jerome Historical District, Yavapai County, Arizona

CALIFORNIA
Bodie State Historical Park, Bodie, California
California State Historical Park, Coloma, California
El Dorado County Museum, Placerville, California
Mariposa County Museum, Mariposa, California
Gene Autry Museum, Los Angeles, California
Johnsville Mining Area, Plumas County, California

COLORADO
South Park City Museum, Fairplay, Colorado
Colorado State Historical Museum, Denver, Colorado

IDAHO
Silver City, Idaho

KANSAS
Dodge City, Kansas

MONTANA
Beaverhead County Museum, Dillon, Montana
Custer National Battlefield, Montana
Nevada City, Montana
Range Riders Museum, Miles City, Montana
Museum of the Plains Indian, Browning, Montana

NEBRASKA
Stuhr Museum of the Prairie Pioneer, Grand Island, Nebraska
Harold Warp Pioneer Village, Minden, Nebraska
Museum of the Fur Trade, Chadron, Nebraska

NEVADA

Nevada State Museum, Carson City, Nevada
Virginia City Historic District, Virginia City, Nevada

NEW MEXICO

Kit Carson Museum, Old Mill Museum, and St James Hotel, Cimarron,
New Mexico

OKLAHOMA

National Cowboy Hall of Fame and Western Heritage Center, Oklahoma City, Oklahoma

OREGON

Jacksonville Museum, Jacksonville, Oregon
End of the Oregon Trail Interpretive Center, Oregon City, Oregon

SOUTH DAKOTA

Deadwood Historic District, Deadwood, South Dakota

UTAH

Silver Reef, Washington County, Utah

WASHINGTON

Port Gamble Historic District, Kitsap County, Washington

WYOMING

Buffalo Bill Historical Center, Cody, Wyoming

Visits to these museums and historical sites would certainly enhance the collector's knowledge of the Old West and provide the opportunity to see vast numbers of artifacts. There is nothing that can take the place of a first-hand visit to these locations. I urge you to seek out other museums and historical areas. If a collector wants a close-up look at genuine articles, museums certainly provide that opportunity. I seem to learn something new at each stop. Tremendous efforts have been made by others to protect and preserve our heritage. They deserve our support!

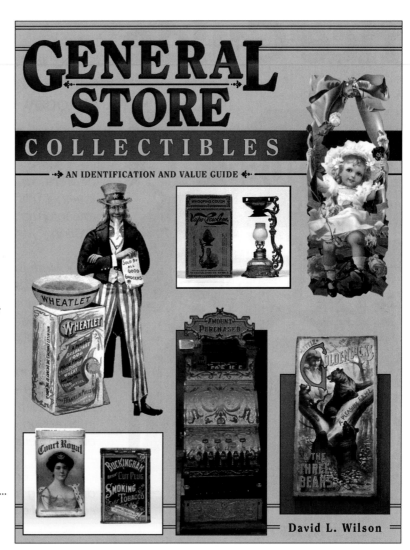